THE WATER PHOENIX

THE WATER PHOENIX

A Memoir of Childhood Abuse, Healing and Forgiveness

RITUPARNA
CHATTERJEE

BLOOMSBURY
NEW DELHI • LONDON • OXFORD • NEW YORK • SYDNEY

BLOOMSBURY INDIA
Bloomsbury Publishing India Pvt. Ltd
Second Floor, LSC Building No. 4, DDA Complex, Pocket C – 6 & 7,
Vasant Kunj, New Delhi 110070

BLOOMSBURY, BLOOMSBURY INDIA and the Diana logo are trademarks of Bloomsbury Publishing Plc

First published in India 2020
This edition published in the Indian subcontinent in 2020

ISBN: HB: 978-93-890-0055-9; eBook: 978-93-890-0057-3

2 4 6 8 10 9 7 5 3 1

Typeset in Fournier MT Std by Manipal Technologies Limited
Printed and bound in India by Replika Press Pvt. Ltd.

MIX
Paper from responsible sources
FSC® C016779
FSC
www.fsc.org

'I am not what happened to me. I am what I choose to become.'

— Carl Gustav Jung

For each child who has been abused.

Contents

PART I

CHILDHOOD

I

The Peepul Tree

'It is the tree of death!' said Manga Kaka. I found this strange coming from a man who dressed in what I was taught to see as the colour of death, white, from head (in a white Nehru cap) to toe (in white Hawaii slippers). The tall peepul tree in my garden did look different with its warty wooden drippings, its mysterious dreadlocks and its time-defying cobwebs. But I never found it spooky. It was simply not of this world. And yet, it seemed that grown-ups were slightly afraid of it, especially on nights like these when thunderstorms raged, and lightning danced furiously across the purple-black night sky my tree climbed into.

Manga Kaka said she was possessed, like a *chudail*. (I wondered how he knew that my tree was a she.) I felt she was possessed too, but only with magic. Whether in a dark thunderstorm or in blinding sunshine, to me my peepul tree was always beautiful. Beautiful like an enchanted grandmother cat. Beautiful in a way that nothing else was in my toddler world — where everything in general was fascinating.

My earliest memory is of waking up in the middle of the night, oblivious to all, and looking out of my parents' bedroom window at my beloved tree, as sounds of rustling surrounded me. I was always fascinated by sounds. For instance, the word Papa birthing the sounds Pup-Pa, which is what my father taught me to call him, even though all the other children I knew called their fathers Paa-Paa. Every time they did that, Baa-baa (*black sheep, have you any wool)* sang in my ears, curling my cheeks into a smile, which the grown-ups saw as sheer cuteness and gushed in vanity, misplacing my joy as being for them, and not for the sound of their roll call names. They loved me instantly.

Perhaps this is why they had named me Saralipi, which means the language of musical notes. I spent a lot of time in and around the kitchen, naturally tuning in to the curry of sounds around me. (As the senses of hearing and taste got mixed up, I spent hours dissecting this puzzle, pulling each flavourful sound apart — the nuttiness of coriander from the zesty warmth of ginger notes, the golden bitterness of turmeric from the comforting sounds of sugar, the fresh hot percussion of green chilies from the aggressive chant-like war cries of red chillies.) On nights like these, I focused on the sounds in the front, the ones that were more mysterious, more alluring, trying to place them together.

I might have been two-and-a-half years old when I first remember doing this, as I lounged around the house in one of my several white sleeveless cotton *tep* frocks that had little sparrows sewn in colourful single stitches at the hem. On most nights, my peepul held its own against a star-studded canvas, looking invincible, with a supernatural strength I had yet to see a human possess. The way I felt about it then was what I was later taught to associate as feelings one has towards one's guardian angel, one's first love, one's first BFF and one's first god.

During the day, I'd spend hours listening to it, whispering secrets into its countless crevices which held ears invisible to all but me. I'd stroke its bumpy rough bark as if it were the soft fur of a giant fluffy dog. One afternoon, after I had finished my ritual of chasing Homeless Peacock on my way back from school, I took a sharp stone and tried to draw a picture of the sun on the peepul's trunk. When my tree cried slow thick white tears, I cried as well, in shame, apologizing profusely for having unknowingly caused it pain. I ran indoors to get first aid supplies and did a quick dressing of Ponds cold cream, a piece of cloth that I found in the kitchen and tape. I offered it my treat for the afternoon, my first taste of *kochuri* — that my school teacher mother had brought from a staff event, safely preserved for me, in the waxy white wrapper of a Good Day biscuit packet from the 1980s. I must have been about four years old.

Old enough to learn how to cough Properly (into a fist), how to kiss loved ones Properly (by brushing lips on their cheeks, as if they were made of paper, and not paint them with spit like dogs were allowed to). Old enough to know that Peacock wasn't really Homeless (it had to keep its address a secret to preserve its ethereal beauty). Old enough to correctly guess that it lived in the topmost part of my peepul, where the leaves were made of gold, merging into a lake of liquid golden sunlight so bright that it blinded those who dared to look. (So, they didn't.) So, it wasn't really a *Peacock* then, was it? It was a *Phoenix!* A Phoenix who lived in the golden waters of its realm. Bored with the beauty of his world he dropped by into mine to say hello.

Year after year, the peepul tree protected us, all of us. Nothing wrong could happen to anybody under its giant umbrella of leaves — which were as large as my frail mother's milk-white palms. They reminded me of the smaller betel leaves my *jethimaa* and Pup-Pa loved to chew on so much, and which too, must therefore possess something magical for grown-ups to get so hooked on to it. Under the dark shade, the lizards who lived in the tree, the rodents who lived at its bottom and the occasional baby goat that strayed in — and that I held captive as my pet for the moment, successfully tempting it with the fibrous carcass of sugarcane cubes I had sucked the juice out of — all of us were safe. I made figurines out of twigs and sticks and left them like a devotee by her trunk.

Because I had not known anything outside of it, I did not know then that this was Eden. What they called Eden. The essence of a perfect, idyllic childhood.

We were in hospitals a lot but again, I did not know that this was not normal. Finally, Maa's health forced us to shift to Calcutta. I made colourful drawings of my peepul tree on postcards for the peepul tree (which I believe Pup-Pa posted for me) so it wouldn't feel lonely or forget me. I had been promised a new cricket bat and ball, so I had no bandwidth for sorrow. Every time Maa went to a hospital on holiday for some days, I was promised a new toy and tons of books. Strangely enough, most of these promises (unlike so many others) were kept.

Calcutta meant lots of bullying by the older cousins and consequently lots of pampering by aunties and nameless grown-ups I had given names to. Most of my aunties were called 'Maa', prefixed with something useful like *Boro* (the kind, elder one), or *Chhoto* (the sweet youngest one), or *Mejo* (the middle, even-tempered one). Or something flattering like *Shona* (golden), or *Mishti* (Bengali sweets), or *Pakhi* (birds), Etsektera. I barely knew my own mother but I experienced her and what having a mother might have been like, in kaleidoscopic fragments through all of these women, many of whom, like the migratory birds they were, left to tend to their own nests.

Then one day, Maa died. As always, nobody told me just like they never told me what exactly was wrong with Maa in the first place. And something was wrong with her for sure because, as I discovered in Calcutta, everybody's mother was not constantly hopping from hospital to hospital on holiday. Nor were they being spoiled with chocolates and toys as I was.

I had to always find things out on my own. From the very beginning. One of the older ones decided to be nice to me and asked me to accompany him to the market to buy plaster of Paris for some project he was doing. (I believe he had to build a bust of this bearded guy called Robi Thakur or Tagore everyone seemed to be so in love with. It was very mysterious and he was everywhere. I couldn't wait to grow up and meet him and ask him why. Perhaps he was a god.) I was thrilled at being acknowledged and felt like a star as I accompanied him. At the shop he suddenly saw something and put an arm on my shoulders, turning me around to ensure I did not look at whatever this something was. Which is exactly why I had to absolutely stop the world and look at whatever this 'something' was. (I had just emptied his old suitcase and sent flying down from the terrace of the old Ancestral House, a lifetime's collection of precious bus tickets and train tickets. Unofficial records of grown-up lives. Children's treasures. It was a fit punishment for excluding me from their games. Perhaps that is why he had finally come to his senses and asked me to accompany him. Still something was rather fishy and reeked of potential conspiracy.)

But there it was — a van as large and rare as a teenage elephant on these narrow *para* streets accustomed to various forms of bikes, rickshaws, cycles, very few tiny cars and the occasional taxi. There was no way to miss it. Nor its contents, which were meant to stay secret but which were given away by its abundance of large glass windows everywhere. Right now, the contents were Maa lying suspiciously asleep, flat with a few strangers surrounding her. She looked so peaceful that she did not look like herself at all.

Upon getting home, a bunch of grown-ups — every grown-up relative I knew and a few others who were new — lay wailing around the wooden tray she lay upon, dressed up as a bride in a traditional scarlet Benaroshi saree. Her face was white, drained of life, but with an artificial red glow reflected in patches here and there from the Benaroshi, which gave me hope.

I ran to her, shook her, tried to wake her up, thereby waking both of us and turning this hallucination lucid.

Mejo Mama whisked me away, imprisoning me in his arms, wetting my frock with his tears. I knew it then. She had died. It was my first epiphany. I screamed like a wild animal, scratching his face, kicking him, letting me go to her. His tears flowed in stinging rivulets through the fresh cuts I had bestowed upon his cheeks. Still, he would not let me go.

Then, Pup-Pa and the rest of them carried her raft-bed on their shoulders and took her away some place to sail. They took me away too, to a cool dark room inside where I cried in somebody's lap, somebody who too, was sobbing, until I fell asleep dreaming of my resting bride mother, her special bed cradled gently by another mother, the Bay of Bengal.

I remembered that the next day was her birthday when she had promised to come home. But it was useless. The day that mattered was today, the 15th of June, 1988.

It was the day I stopped trusting grown-ups — Important Lesson No. 1.

2

The Nameless Tree

The world I knew had become unrecognizable, as if painted with an invisible coat of Bizarre. A function named Shraad to honour the spirit of the recently dead brought everybody together again. But this was the first GetTwoTogether where nobody was celebrating anything. They were in a daze, floating as if in a collective dream. Is this how dead people live? Were they the WalkingBreathingDead then? It was not just that gloom had deposited itself all over the Ancestral House, settling as maroon iron sediments in its utensils, stains which could not be washed off, and entered us as we ate and drank in them. It was something more, which I couldn't place, which had turned everything foreign. Pup-Pa for instance, had suddenly become unrecognizable, an alien. Having shaved his head, he now resembled Humpty Dumpty wearing a white cotton cloth (which he informed me was called a *dhooti*) and carrying a Wand (which was really a NotSoSpecial stick) everywhere which made him look more like a child than me.

What was especially weird was when we went visiting hospitals and public places and he had to speak. His voice travelled from a deep, hollow *haandi* pot inside of him, a deep, hollow iron-stained *haandi* pot.

We continued to visit hospitals albeit for different reasons revolving around my brief history on this planet. MultipleSources informed me that unlike most babies, I was born not crying but coughing into the world. *This* was slightly unusual. And the cause for *This* had just been discovered. I had a hole in my heart, in the wall which separated the clean blood from the dirty blood. So, it got mixed up, making it hard to breathe while my chest burned from activities natural to a child. Running or jumping. (Yet another reason why I developed special pleasures like picnics with my tree, eating up books and stories and seeing things that most people did not see — for example, the rather obvious extraordinariness of my tree). Along with the recently acquired '*Maahaara*' (motherless) title, my recently discovered defective heart got me even more attention. I knew this was unnecessary but grown-ups had a penchant for the dramatic. It was their way of dealing with a reality they themselves had sucked the magic out of. As always, the truth was obvious. InPlainSight. As always, grown-ups (and those whom they had successfully managed to influence with their boring ways) were oblivious to it. The hole in my heart was a tunnel through which a mysterious superpower would manifest anytime! Perhaps when I was grown up, perhaps sooner. I was not 100 per cent sure about the timing. But I was 100 per cent sure it would happen. Definitely! If you listened carefully, you could hear it murmuring its way in already. The doctors (being grown-ups after all) had misdiagnosed *This* magical sound as something they called a heart murmur and which, judging from their (dramatically) tragic tones, they deemed to be a catastrophe.

They painted my chest with a translucent paint which had Vicks VapoRub's consistency and coldness but not its strong camphor scent. I wished they'd wait a bit! I needed to do a critical experiment confirming whether light passed through this special gooey balm or not. But they were too fast for any scientific observations. Instead, they stuck stickers and wires all over me and asked me to answer stupid questions — the name of my school, names of my dolls (I didn't have any), how I was feeling (annoyed but obviously I said fine), Etsektera. My answers created endless ugly squiggles on a tiny TV screen, which was certainly a language script because the nurses and doctors read it with great interest.

These tests, which I was told measured the electrical activity in my heart, became routine. (My heart had electricity! How cool was that! Just like a fridge or a TV or an iron, so long as you plugged it in, which they did with some wires that didn't hurt at all. Yet another promising sign of my future superpower, which could manifest anytime!) So did boring photographs of my insides, under my skin and mutton called X-rays, which very soon piled up into a little tower. So did elevator rides which were a total treat.

Upon returning, I checked and confirmed that light did not pass through Vicks or gum, both doppelgangers of that gooey thing. However, due to the thoughtless speed of nurses in all the hospitals I visited at the time and over the years, I never found out whether light passed through the nameless balm, which made visible the electric power of hearts. This will always remain one of my life's GreatestRegrets.

Important Lesson No. 2: Seize your experiments out of the clutches of grown-ups. (Or live with a collection of GreatestRegrets.)

The cloud of gloom carried us gently, finally making a soft landing back home in Nandurbar where everything was very quiet, very still.

Nobody talked about it. I barely knew her. In fact, we had spent such little time together that my memories of her more or less matched the total number of fingers I had. Memories like:

1. Forcing me into her lap in the backyard while Manga Kaka and other *kakas* gently pinned down my limbs (only as 100 per cent necessary,) so I could be fed freshly squeezed neem juice. The most bitter and ghastly thing on Earth!
2. Watering the tiny papaya tree, tomatoes and other plants in the backyard together.
3. Her cutting out pretty diamond shapes in dough to be turned into delicious *kucho nimki*. My eleventh favourite food!
4. Using glasses to cut out circles to fry up *loochis* rounder than the moon while I watched the neat rows of Kissan jam jars and Farex and Lactogen tins she had recycled to hold spices, lentils, Etsektera.
5. Making me lie down and using a *jhinook* to feed me milk. Yuck!

6. Forcing me to finish studies on Sunday mornings super fast. (Otherwise I couldn't watch He Man, thereby adding to GreatestRegrets.)
7. Teaching me to kiss properly on the cheek without licking, spitting or biting.
8. Teaching me to cough politely, with my fist covering my cough.
9. Running to her as I tripped over the wire of the hot iron (Manga Kaka was ironing clothes on the floor) and got a mild shock and burn and her holding me and then cheering me up with a paper boat she made magically out of thin air.
10. Yelling at the ants who had bitten my toes, where she applied Boroline. Or yelling at the ground or whoever else (whatever object) had dared to hurt me, threatening them with the worst fate ever.
11. Similarly yelling at Pup-Pa and whisking me away into her arms when he slapped me for the first time. (Because I'd answered 2+2=3.)
12. Propping me on her knees while she lay down and rocking me while simultaneously rolling her eyelids up to turn into a *petni* with orange eyes (the true colour of the sun and the sun-lake where the Peacock/Phoenix lived) scaring the daylights out of me!
13. Her hiding and crying. When I asked her what had happened, her holding me tight and crying even more.

That's it! More or less. Yet, I ached for her in a way that was new to me, with a pain I had not known before.

It was after all, my very first experience with death. Nobody could hide the void she left behind either, not Pup-Pa, not Manga Kaka and certainly not our railway bungalow in Nandurbar.

Upon returning, I was renamed Rituparna. Like the series of events unfolding, this too, was random and sudden for me but apparently (as MultipleSources informed me) it was her idea. I was annoyed to have to learn to spell and practise writing my name all over again, especially in cursive. (Because this brought extra slaps from Pup-Pa, with no Maa to whisk me away.) But oh, how fitting it was to be named after the process of how leaves change from season to season! The cycle of birth, growth, death, rebirth, repeat — a metaphor for life itself. It was fitting because my fascination for sounds had faded, only to be replaced with an obsession for foliage — not just of my own beloved peepul, but that of every tree, bush, shoot and weed I encountered. (I did not know then that this would turn into an addiction that would last a lifetime.)

My name being changed to one about trees should have brought me even closer with my beloved pet peepul. But in our long-distance relationship, my tree had changed. Somehow, in that space which we didn't know existed before because oblivious to us and perhaps even to her, Maa had somehow filled it, my own love for my tree had changed. I could no longer find myself in her. Had death made me grow up? Was I too, the WalkingBreathingDead now?

As Pup-Pa, aided by Manga Kaka and a tiny army of loving domestic staff, struggled to look after me amidst his multiple work trips and transfers, my education threatened to *Sooeeside* (a needle on the side). And so, as it happens in old Hindi movies, I was shipped off to a relative. It seemed alright enough. After the triple loss of Maa, my name and my pet peepul, there was nothing left for me in Nandurbar. I waved goodbye to my beloved nameless tree and drowned myself in the legal drug that is books, emerging hazy and sedated from their world only when I had arrived.

Getting into the big Ambassador taxi to reach my aunty's house in a dusty, small town in Central India was the beginning of the adventure. I assumed I'd continue to be treated like royalty by them, because it was all I had ever known. Pup-Pa left with a smile, happy to see me so excited. The next day when I did not finish my lunch and instead painted my steel plate with most of the bland dal, rice and especially insipid veggies, explaining they were crumbs, I was asked with a stern politeness foreign to me, to never repeat it again.

Important Lesson No.3: The party was over.

I did not know then that this was the beginning of Hell.

My aunt's two boys (let's call the older one Devil No. 1 and the younger one Devil No. 2) were rambunctious on good days and absolute terrors on bad days. She often ran around the house in a trance of rage, chasing the older one with a rolling pin while he dodged her and pleaded for mercy calling her *Maaji*. It looked like a sport. It was also very amusing because it was the first time I had seen a

Bengali child address their mother in the way of the North Indian locals.

Those were the few peaceful days. On most days I did not know what condition I'd wake up in. One morning I woke up with my hands tied up. On another, I was kicked awake because apparently the giggling culprit, Devil No. 2, who was pretending to be asleep, was playing soccer in his sleep. On yet another, I woke up with cocoa powder in my hair and on my face and then being punished after the culprits accused me of creating a mess and stealing the precious ingredients of the cake that was to be made later and successfully managed to convince the authorities that I had committed the crime. Looking at the huge mess she had to clean up on a school morning, she naturally lost it. Even then, my six-year-old heart (WholeHeartWithaHole) went out to her. My beloved books disappeared, mysteriously reappearing days later with the names of the boys written in as the owners. It wasn't that they ever read them, but it was good to have a mouse to play with. I went to the bathroom to cry only to discover that I had been locked in with my greatest terror ever — a big fat gecko. I screamed and screamed and screamed, pleading to be let out. I was breathless. My face felt hot. I knew I'd die any minute, which I did not mind, but I did not want to die with a lizard on me. Only when my aunt yelled from the kitchen that the boys stop this at once, did they let me out. When I finally was, I summoned the strength to walk into the balcony for fresh air where invisible hands gently pushed me into a tall cactus, the balcony's only living resident. It apologized with its long line-like sad cactus eyes and mouth. We, the two friendless ones in this flat, became friends.

Somewhere in this daily drama, I lost my confidence, my lust for magic and my essence. School was the only place which brought some relief but also unimaginable shock to see these devil brothers turn into docile darlings and teachers' pets, excelling in everything from academia to sport to extracurriculars. Devil No. 1 was a monitor or captain or something like that and I watched in shock as he became the picture of the good kid everyone was supposed to aspire to, holding the flag at assembly, commanding marches Etsektera. The sun added to his glory, bouncing off the metal badge on his dark green school blazer.

One afternoon, they somehow caught hold of a mysterious treasure — an umbrella-shaped contraption with spokes, which was the size of both of my palms put together. Devil No. 1 said it was a magnet from an old radio. To me, it might as well have been a communication device from another planet. Of course, they didn't share it. I was grateful for the peace. Still, I couldn't help noticing how lovingly their two heads were bent over it together, inventing deep scientific theories and games around this special magnet. During evenings each of them picked up a *phoring* (cricket) in their fingers and had them shake hands, interact, Etsektera, until finally letting them go. Their bond filled me with deep envy and a painful awareness of just how alone I was. I ran to the balcony to my cactus friend.

I did not know at what moment my predators would attack. But it was always at the house, never at school or while playing with other children. I'd have given anything to trade places with prey animals like zebra or deer. Because:

1) They had their herd. I only had a cactus.
2) When not hungry, their predators left them alone. My predators were never satiated.

I lived in constant terror, with my every move being watched. Naturally, this powerlessness turned into hate. One day, when my paan-loving *jethima* was visiting, we walked to a nearby place, a temple or a shopping complex. I had raced slightly ahead, grateful for a few moments of solitude even though it was a good day. It always was, when relatives visited. I discovered that the road ended at a bumpy dusty area called a ConstructionArea. It was very cool with its bamboo poles on mud and little dug up wells of water. To my first-grader self, it looked deep enough to kill someone. An egg hatched in my head, birthing a plot to end my misery. When everybody came close, I pushed the older brother into the well, convinced he would drown. Definitely! One hundred per cent. It was my first moment of victory, my first step out of powerlessness. A loud, shrill laugh of victory started in my heart (WholeHeartWithaHole) and escaped out of my mouth as a roar. So this is how they feel when they bully me, I thought, savouring the cruel joy that shook me. My aunts froze in shock... Until his screams woke them up. They hitched up their sarees and helped him out. Unfortunately, it was not a well but a huge puddle and so, he lived. One hundred per cent. Not only lived, he came out and immediately, pushed me in. I being shorter, had a greater chance of drowning. One hundred per cent. He got a tight slap, to my delight, as my disturbed aunties pulled me out. The hot sun quickly dried us up. His nylon clothing barely had any traces while my pretty cotton frock had sullied shamefully with mud and defeat.

I did not ever try to fight back after that. Life went on. Pup-Pa when he visited, always brought books and plum cake. He dismissed my fears saying it was just a classic case of childhood. He then joked fondly about how the two devils had gone on their dad (let's call him P) and his poor, sweet, loving sister, my aunt (it's time we name her, so let's call her M) had to bear with them. He spent more time with the two devils, bonding with them over sport, spoiling them silly buying them footballs and cricket bats, loving them more while I became quieter and quieter, sneaking into corners, grateful to be left alone with new books. I tried to finish them as soon as I could lest I be robbed of what was mine yet again. (Later I'd find that Pup-Pa loved all other children more than me. Even later, I'd find that all parents loved other children more than their own, perhaps out of good manners, but it evened things out, greatly shortening the world's list of GreatestRegrets.)

They say you attract what you have become. I had become only one thing: prey. 24X7, walking, school-going, solitude-loving, frock-wearing, book-devouring, ice cream-loving prey. And just like guilt attracts punishment, preys attract predators.

I wish I knew this then. Life might have turned out different.

3

The Swimming Pool

What is a family without its weekend traditions? On Sunday mornings P packed his delighted sons onto his blue-grey Bajaj scooter and they drove off to the public swimming pool, leaving a trail of laughter in the scooter's smoke. M stayed at home, getting a desperately needed break. On one such morning, thanks to my glaring lack of extracurricular activities, I was told to accompany P and the boys. I stood in front of the scooter, adding to the picture postcard-perfect Happy Family moment. Pup-Pa was around, which meant that the devils were busy because he loved them more, because he laughed with them, because he bought footballs and played football with them. During these rare times, the blue-grey Bajaj's laughter-filled smoke mingled with the white-grey incense M lit every evening, teaching my first-grader mind the Smell of Relief. The smoke of happiness filled everybody's lungs, infecting everyone, gifting my father (who loved other children more) the illusion that I was happy. The Smell of Relief ran in spirals, delivering different meanings to each breather — for me, it meant I could take a break from being prey.

We reached early and sat by the cement bench circling a huge nameless tree with large fleshy leaves, each the size of a sumo wrestler's palm. I smiled at the tree. The devils laughed at my eccentricity. Its height and strength reminded me of my peepul, a hazy memory from a past life.

P tore a few and gave them to us, asking us to eat them, saying it was a medicinal tree that detoxifies the body and increases appetite. We grimaced at the surprisingly strong (sumo-wrestler-strong) sourness of the leaves. It was one of the rare times when Devil No. 1 and Devil No. 2 and I did something together.

The devils already knew how to swim. At age 11, Devil No. 1 was a bit of a champion, diving beautifully off the diving board at the deep end while everyone watched, impressed. Devil No. 2 hoped to be him eventually and in the meantime practised, cannonballing noisily in the children's section, splashing everyone outside generously until they were soaked. I watched them and others and before I knew it I had been pushed into the water, my forehead hitting the tiled floor, my lungs filling with chlorine water. Luckily this was the shallow children's end, so I emerged immediately — coughing, gasping and chiding myself for not being my usual hyper alert self. How dare I assume I would be safe!

Nobody paid any attention to the gash on my temple. Children get cuts and bruises all the time anyway. It dried up, scabbing at the speed of a train leaving a station.

Submerged in the joys of cannonballing, Devil No. 2 lost interest in me. Devil No. 1 was too busy showing off. The grown-ups were busy chatting, swimming, fussing over Devil No. 1's stellar performance, encouraging him to excel further, and other stuff grown-ups do. I was delightfully left alone. The Smell of Relief bathed me, filling my cautious shadow with new courage. After being completely and absolutely 100 per cent, 500 per cent sure that I was safe and indeed forgotten, I grabbed one of the many 'tubes', which is what everyone called those tire-shaped floating devices that lay scattered around. I wore it at my waist and stepped into the water for the first time.

The water embraced me, floating me around gently. The Feeling of Love. It was exhilarating. I remembered a freedom I had not felt in so long, that I had forgotten it even existed. From then onwards, I loved the pool like Devil No.1 and Devil No.2 but for completely different reasons. I was left alone, free to do whatever the Hell I wanted to, for a change. I decided to take this precious piece of freedom to a whole new level by choosing to be someone else. The privileges of actors. I took graceful strokes in the safety of my tube because I was a mermaid or a water fairy, hanging out in her backyard. Soon, I felt brave enough to step out of the tube and hold it in front of me, gracefully moving in dance-like movements, because I was another kind of a fairy and my flotation device was actually an enchanted pitcher made of gold which I was filling up with magic dust to take back home with me. My home with Homeless Peacock who lived in the liquid golden realm at the top of my peepul and who really was a Phoenix, a Water Phoenix.

Pup-Pa left. I began to live for Sundays and these slices of Heaven they brought. The Smell of Relief. The Feeling of Love.

I began to venture into the middle section of the pool. Most of the children here knew how to swim. But I was confident in my armour, my tube. That is, until the day when somebody pulled my tube away and another pair of hands pushed my legs under. I gasped, terrified, knowing I wouldn't survive. My body felt separate from me as I entered a tunnel of darkness, immediately blinded by what appeared like liquid light. Tall shadowy figures which looked like they were made of light blue X-rays surrounded me. And then, what seemed to be a completely different pair of hands pushed my buttocks forcefully — making me realize I was back in my body — towards the pool stairs. Gratefully, I grabbed the steps and the railing and stepped out gasping, coughing, crying in shock.

Everything happened in a sequence and was over in what seemed like a minute. When I looked at the pool, it looked like a normal pool of human beings, mostly children. Had I just imagined the whole thing up? My burning lungs and throat convinced me that I hadn't.

Who had pushed me? Who had saved me? I never found out. Was it the devils? I didn't know for sure, so I could not accuse them.

'Tata, Pool,' I said sadly, grateful for its brief gift of freedom, which was now over because I had to be on my guard again.

P's voice called me, asking me to come with him to get cleaned up and changed. This was routine. We were small children. It was usually P who bathed us, ensuring that he had doused us in mustard oil before the bath and we stood in the sun long enough for the goodness to sink into our bodies before he washed us off. I was used to having zero time to recover from shocks and get on with whatever life demanded of me. So I followed him as if everything were normal. Nobody in the world knew, and I myself wouldn't realize until my third decade, that I had just had an NDE (near-death experience).

In a daze, I followed P to the bathrooms beyond the lockers. He had grabbed a towel and soap and a bathroom at the end of a row of empty bathrooms. He undressed me as usual and turned on the shower, scrubbing me with the kind of force necessary in cleaning a stubborn dirty pot. I was certain the green soap would make green suds but white bubbles appeared. It was magic! My eyes had widened, processing this little wonder when I was asked to close them. The white bubbles were harshly rubbed into them. The smile on my face had not even stretched completely when a sharp pain shot through my very being. 'Don't open your eyes,' P warned. But how could I not when I was in so much pain? Immediately the soap stung my eyes and I screamed. P slapped me. 'What did I tell you? Don't open your eyes. You naughty girl. Stop screaming now.'

As always, I obeyed.

I cried softly with the soap burning my eyes and the pain tearing through me. I focused on watching with my eyes closed, tracing the pain through to the source. Without my realizing it, my hand intuitively followed touching the source of the pain. It turned out to be something soft, yet hard, a fleshy cylinder-like object had entered where I would normally pee from and never touch otherwise. Instinctively, I hit it, trying to remove it like a weak magnet from a metal door and unknowingly pinched it in the process. An even harder slap on my burning wet cheek. That's when I realized it was P. And he was clearly doing something he wasn't supposed to do.

As always, I obeyed.

Unknown to me and even to himself, P planted a Tentacle in me. Over the years, this foreign Tentacle would branch out, slowly revealing its alien tentacular characteristics in places completely unrelated, swallowing me whole, alive from my own insides. But I did not know that then. And of course, neither did he.

He cleaned me up, washing me with warm water. A favourite soap jingle ran in a loop in my head.

Chehre ki sundertaa ko nikharta HAMAM.

He dried and dressed me. As I waited, by the pool, he got the boys, bathed, dried and dressed them. I did not know then that I would always be afraid of swimming. That somehow, I would continue to use that soap. That I would not step into a pool for the next 22 years. That I would be the odd Bengali who hated anything mustard (the Smell of Abuse) for two decades. That all green soaps gave white suds.

We went back home as if it were just another day.

I had just beaten death and been raped. All in one day.

4

Life as Prey

How I wished for a crystal ball to tell me that *It* would never happen again. (Because *It* did not! *It* never did — not on any of the many afternoons when P massaged us with pungent mustard oil before leaving us to wander around in the backyard with our greasy, stinky skins soaking in the goodness of the sun before he bathed us. *It* never happened during bath time ever again, even as the five thousand pores on my skin kept vigil. Thousands of wide-awake eyes. *It* never happened during the countless times I was left alone with P in or out of the house.)

But how could I have known this? So, I lived in continuous fright, battling with insomnia at the tender age of six, kept awake by my overwhelming need to stay alert at all times. I did not know then that this insomnia would be my constant companion — almost like my partner in an everlasting fairy-tale wedding, faithful to me till the end of my living days. I never slept peacefully again — not unless I was sedated.

My medical vocabulary grew by leaps and bounds. I learnt words like sedated, kneemokneeah, skizzofreneeah, earthraytees, diareeah, diabeetees, gastraytees, deemenshia, kidknee stones… I loved to be around grown-ups, listening in to their talk. They were safe to be with. All the Bengali grown-ups I knew loved to talk about their ailments and exchange stories of illness that were tinged with melodrama. I suppose that was because of the attention that talk of their illnesses brought for them. This attention must have felt like love to them. They didn't stop just at illness though and discussed death with equal fervour. Was it for the relief and excitement that the concept of death held? Otherwise, their lives seemed boring and they always complained of being tired.

The adults saw me perpetually drowned in the world of books. Would that make me like a skizzofrenik living in her own world who, therefore, was as harmless to them as a plant in the living room? But children keep their eyes and ears open. I was the notorious fly on the wall, lapping up nectars of information, especially ones I was not supposed to be lapping up at all. One day, I learned a new word — *call-era*. It sounded like a mysterious illness and from the way the adults talked about it, it did not appear to have anything to do with speech, sound or hearing, or whatever faculties one used in the act of calling anybody. It must be *kolera* then, I decided. I was already beginning to learn that English was not a phonetic language like Bengali, Hindi or Marathi. *Kolera* sounded fascinating and I could think of nothing else.

When Pup-Pa visited us for Christmas holidays, he brought a cake baked in the shape of a house. The snow on its roof was made of white icing. 'Pup-Pa, this house looks like the witch's house from *Hansel and Gretel*,' I said. He smiled. He looked pleased. I did not want to blot out his happiness by telling him that I felt as if I were being imprisoned. That I felt like a captive child in the house. That a horrible, witch-like Tentacle was eating up my insides. Instead, I focussed on making him happier by asking him a question because he loved me asking questions. And finally, I had the chance to get this nagging one out of my head — 'Pup-Pa, what's *kolera*?' His smile widened. He did not ask me where I had heard it. All he said was, 'That's a big word. What's the spelling?' I took a pencil and wrote in my notebook: *k o l e r a*. He laughed and, grabbing my pencil, wrote the correct spelling: *c h o l e r a*. I ran off as just then, the devils arrived. But it was okay. I did not need an answer as now I could look it up in the dictionary. I had been taught how to use it, but I still found it overwhelming. Grown-ups especially seemed to love me peering into it.

After several attempts, I finally found it — *c h o l e r a*: the dictionary said it was *an infectious and often fatal bacterial disease of the small intestine, typically contracted from infected water supplies and causing severe vomiting and diarrhoea*. It sounded so complicated. I knew *infectious*, but looked up the next big word, *fatal* — causing death. How interesting. I wished they'd all die of *kolera*, sorry *cholera*. I made up a curse, my very first, cursing the devils and P to catch a *cholera* as soon as possible and die of it — as soon as possible.

Nobody died of anything. Nobody even caught anything. Instead, I got the rashes — my punishment for cursing. It turned out that I had caught measles. I was quickly bundled out of the room I slept in with the devils, and moved to another room where M slept with me at night. It turned out to be the best thing to ever happen to me! I was left alone, and I was naturally safe, for the first time. Being sick, especially with new stuff, was awesome! It was an added bonus. No wonder grown-ups were obsessed with illness — the stranger, the better. I reveled in the luxury of feeling safe. I was free to do anything.

How I wished that I'd never get better! In the days of my measles, I had a ton of time to ponder over life's endless mysteries:

1. Why did stray dogs dig deep pits in new mountains of sand in the outdoors for themselves to sit and sleep in?
2. Was the abandoned B-Type flat in the colony with rags hanging from the branches on its trees really haunted?
3. What did doctors do in an operation? Was it what the butcher did to chickens and goats?
4. When I pressed the button, how did water spurt out of the plastic jewel in the center of my plastic *pichkari*?
5. What if we buried teeth that fell out and watered them? Would they grow into huge ivory tusk trees that we could sell for millions?
6. Would all the snot in the world together create a city that could become a creche for tadpoles while their parents went to work?
7. Preeti Ma'am's favourite student was a boy. Why? (Preeti Ma'am was my *kathak* teacher.)
8. Why was a haircut called a boy-cut when both girls and boys got them? Who had decided this?
9. What would happen if nobody ever cut their hair? Would we live in a forest of soft hair with houses and beddings and rooms of soft hair?

10. *Buddhi ka baal* — cotton candy — was made of neither hair nor cotton. Then what was it made of? And how was it made?
11. Why had the pool incident happened? Who had pushed me? Who had saved me?
12. Why had P done what he had done?

Maybe he was just plain curious, I concluded in his defence. I felt like a lab rat, not knowing when an awful foreign thing would be injected into me just because some scientist or P felt curious that day.

Living as prey had instilled within me, a deep desire for safety. I learned to look for the Smell of Relief. I found it in cupboards, behind doors, in the run-down, abandoned and supposedly haunted B-Type flat. How bad could ghosts be, anyway! Maybe, I could read to them. Maybe, if they remembered how to read, we could even read together.

Life as prey taught me to value freedom. Freedom was priceless, and it allowed you to do little things and to just 'be'. Threat was constant, a pregnant cloud in an overcast sky ready to burst mercilessly anytime, like a time bomb ticking away, each moment bringing me closer to an unknown disaster. Threat taught me to truly appreciate the little things, to look for the subtle stuff. I did not know then how huge a gift this was — a gift that would last me a lifetime. A gift that would save my life in spite of the almighty Tentacle. Like right now, I was very, very, very grateful to be sick. It was like being in Paradise. I relished every bit of it because I knew it wouldn't last forever.

Health returned. And with it came the abuse, with the certainty of the sun rising every morning. The days blurred into patterns of terror and peace, as constant as the rhythm of the seesaw in a playground. Fascination and horror blended together inside and outside of the house. For the first time, I saw a chameleon changing colours in a dry cement drain with high walls on either side. Theirs was the first kitchen I saw, where instead of a gas stove there was a smart electric stove. I stood transfixed by its white coils, knowing it was like a coiled, sleeping snake. The coils turned red, then white, then red again, following a rhythm of their own. The devils appeared in the kitchen, keen to make their own observations. They wanted to see if I'd turn into a *bhutta*. But the countertop was too high, and I was too short and I was saved. They were just teasing, but I couldn't help screaming in shock. M, who had just left the kitchen for a minute, returned, and chased them away with the threat of a good beating.

Casually, P told the neighbours about my impressive command over English grammar at such a young age and my insatiable lust for reading. They responded with dutiful '*Wows*', which echoed everywhere. Criticism had so far, surrounded me, and abuse had drowned me. Praise had been as rare as rain in the desert. I drank it up like a thirsty traveller, smiling for the rest of the day. But later, P accosted me in the small abandoned corridor between the two bedrooms and I almost choked in fear as he shot in his spear-like tongue into my throat. He pulled at my non-existent breasts. It all happened in an instant, and just as quickly, he walked off. I felt as if unable to breathe, and gasped. Had this really happened in the past few seconds? I was sure my mouth was bleeding. 'No!' said the mirror politely. 'Yes!' screamed my burning and livid chest. Its ribs, protectors of life-giving organs, throbbed in a painful chorus.

P's behaviour was, indeed, baffling! Hadn't he just abused and hurt me? But he often yelled at his boys for troubling me. He was mostly kind to me — even helping Pup-Pa out with Etsektera grown-up stuff and took care of me, together with M. On my birthday, he had once bought me a dress I had loved — a bright orange knee-length sleeveless frock with black bows on the shoulders. A huge glittery butterfly at the central part of the bottom hem was the only embellishment on the otherwise plain dress. It had been my favourite for many years. Whenever a baby bird, a fledgling, fell from the nest its stubborn parents kept making in the devils' home, P would pick it up, nurse it till it was stronger and would then return it gently to its home.

Mythological stories and legends, and fairy tales that grown-ups told children seemed crystal clear about what was good and what was evil, what was right and what was wrong. They knew their stuff. But despite them influencing me so hugely, I could not use their lens to separate good from evil, black from white, protector from predator, provider from robber, love from abuse. Perhaps, such confidence, such certain clarity, was true only in stories. In real life, everything was jumbled up into one endless swimming pool where all colours were mixed up together.

I did not have the luxury of being dazed. M called me and handed over to me a book and a pencil, asking me to finish some math work before I met her again to recite my multiplication tables. I finished and went promptly to the kitchen where she was frying some delicious somethings in a *kadhai* full of golden oil, over the same electric stove that could have turned me into *bhutta*. I stepped back cautiously, keeping my distance, reminding myself not to allow the coils' hypnotic beauty to take hold of me.

Satisfied with my homework, M asked me to recite the tables. They got tougher after 5, but I managed to smoothly make it to 8. 'Go on,' M said. I did so, slowly, carefully:

8 ones are 8
8 twos are 16
8 threes are 20
8 fours are 32
8 fives are 40
8 sixes are…

'Stop!' M said, putting down her steel *khunti* on the countertop and walking towards the bedroom. I followed her next to the open cupboard where, not so long ago, she had given me a basic lesson in folding clothes. I looked proudly at the tiny pile of neatly folded garments on the second-lowest shelf. This, too, was a mission I had accomplished successfully. I looked up, expecting at least a hint of praise, or another echo of *'Wows'*. Instead, I was asked to repeat the multiplication tables from 8 onwards. I obeyed:

8 ones are 8
8 twos are 16

8 threes are 20
8 fours are 32
8 fives are 40
8 sixes are 48

'Stop!' she commanded. In my bladder, my nervousness turned to fear. 'Are you sure?' I nodded again. 'Something's amiss. Try again,' she said. Meditating on the little column of clothes, in the hope for clues, I slowly repeated the exact version of the table yet again. It was the only one I knew. All of a sudden, she pulled my hair, as if it had to be contained into a fountain, then pushed me down to the hard floor. When I looked up, I saw the shock that should have been mine reflected on M's face. I felt suddenly betrayed. While she hit the devils often enough, she had never hit me before. M was the only one I loved in that House of Fears.

Something warm dripped slowly down from my temple. Instinctively, my hands reached out to touch it and my eyes, which had never seen so much of it ever before, took in the beautiful bright colour of the blood on my fingertips.

M's face turned into a canvas of emotions: guilt, fear, shock and shame reflected on her face. The room filled up with her extreme exhaustion and sense of powerlessness. I felt bad for her. Perhaps, also because the wound on the forehead that she was now inspecting did not hurt at all — nothing compared to the invisible ones that P had inflicted (and the Tentacle he had implanted). That wound overshadowed this one completely.

'If people ask how you got hurt, just say, "I was running around playing with my brothers and hurt myself on the bedpost",' she said quietly after dressing my wound.

As always, I obeyed. My blood too, from that point onwards, obeyed inaudible, often unspoken orders and dried up.

Was obedience the reason why I suffered so regularly? Or was it because I simply did not care? I wondered about this often. Soon after, M told her version of events to a curious neighbour who happened to drop by just then. 'Poor thing!' she exclaimed, before they continued with their conversation. This answer was regurgitated successfully to other curious adults. It was surprising how easily grown-ups believed the lies told by other grown-ups. Yet children were questioned and often punished for smaller lies.

In the few seconds of privacy I had, mostly in the bathroom, I used pencils, pens, sticks, and whatever tools I could smuggle inside to undress and press the wound, causing it to bleed again — bleed and bleed and bleed until no more blood was left to reach my brain — or so, I reasoned. It was my first suicide attempt, the suicide attempt of a six-year-old. It was simply too innocent to be successful.

The fairy tales I escaped into kept my spirit alive, allowing me to experience a sense of calm I did not know I needed so desperately. Like fruit, my make-believe world of stories preserved and nourished me to withstand the Tentacle's rot that was spreading inside me, consuming me.

That evening, P and M took us to the shopping centre. They bought me a stylish rainbow striped white Baggy Sweater and P even entertained my toddler dream of owning squeaky shoes, the kinds that announced the wearer's arrival, step-by-step as she approached regally like a princess, loved by one and all. The shopkeeper explained how these were only for kids half my size. I time-travelled to my toddler self, wearing squeaky shoes under the peepul with Maa and Pup-Pa and Manga Kaka, Homeless Peacock/Water Phoenix looking from above — and the Smell of Relief everywhere. Squeak-squeak went my shoes — the Sound of Love.

I vowed to never let the years pass by again. P took us to a place called The Coffee House. It smelled of elegance, polite, red-turbaned, white-uniformed waiters filling the place with a Sense of Posh. Like so many firsts, P bought me my first paper dosa. Bending my head to the side, I peered into the beautiful rice paper tunnel, its insides gritty, yet so much like the insides of my closed eyelids, the colour of the sun and the realms it ruled, the land of Homeless Peacock/Water Phoenix. The tunnel magically and instantly revealed its invisible secrets to me, only me. I ate it up like Hanuman had once tried to eat the sun.

One morning when Devil No.2 was indulging in his usual game of ragging me, some of the many burning embers inside me burst like a time bomb. Boom! I bit his arm hard like the hunted wild animal I had been forced to become, shocking the daylights out of both him and me. He screamed to be rescued. P rushed him to the hospital for a tetanus shot — just in case. It was the first time I had felt so powerful. Although briefly, I had managed to protect myself. (And I received neither punishment nor scolding for this act of cruelty. Not even one stern look.) Could I try the same behaviour with a grown-up? With P? Could I be so powerful?

I never did find out. Old habits resurfaced soon enough and I went back to living as prey, for what felt like a lifetime. My only escape was time travel, and that helped, but only temporarily. Gradually, I lost whatever confidence or sense of self I had. Fear became the only way of life I knew now, and life itself was like an endless panic attack. I hid behind doors, hyper-vigilant, ever ready to catch the slightest movement that might signify a potential attack. Sometimes, I would react to even the sound of the passing breeze that would gently sway the door.

Pup-Pa had an eccentric brother who unexpectedly came to visit. He was kind, intuitive, but lived mostly in his own world. He even talked to himself. There was no official diagnosis on him, but my 'grown-up self' believed he was on some spectrum of mental illness, perhaps a form of autism. When he heard me whimpering like a wounded kitten, he peered from behind the door and smiled quietly at me. Then, he stroked my head and walked off. But he had noticed that this sense of fright he had witnessed in me was more than just a one-off incident, that it was my way of existing. It had taken a 'special needs' person to see what was always InPlainSight.

Soon after, Pup-Pa arrived, bringing along with him, his regular air of celebration. But this time, my sense of celebration was greater, if not the greatest in the world. I was to pack my things and leave with him. At once! I was so happy, I thought I was flying. I didn't look back even once, completely overwhelmed by the Smell of Relief.

Many years later, Pup-Pa told me how thankful he was to his eccentric brother who had told him bluntly, 'Your daughter is being eaten alive over there. She's being finished, frightened out of her wits. Get her before it's too late.' He had saved my life.

Angels come in many forms, almost always without wings and halos, but sometimes they are so ordinary and so familiar that we fail to recognize them until years pass. I did not realize that this *jethu* — UndiagnosedAutisticUncle — the family's underdog, whom everyone had no expectations from, had given me a second life. I found this out only several years after his early death. I never got the chance to thank him.

Another angel would soon enter my life. And this time, I would recognize her immediately.

5

My Mothers and I

Back in Nandurbar, when I asked once to go discover what lay beyond our regular park, Manga Kaka said, 'Not there. *Banjaras* are there.' I knew the rest. There were gypsies. Like bearded men, *chudails*, circus folk, besides a long list of other interesting creatures — all joined together like multicoloured beads on a necklace strung together by the fact that they were strangers — strangers who took away little children in their *jholas*.

Once upon a time, when my peepul was still mine, Manga Kaka had called her a *chudail*. Did this mean that *chudails*, peepuls and gypsies, all belonged to one species? That they could transform like *icchadhari naags* (shape-shifting cobras)? So, the police could never ever catch these kidnappers of kids because they didn't quite know who they were looking for. And the fact that they had *jholas* did not really qualify them as kidnappers, did it?

I longed to go there not just because I had been specifically forbidden to do so, but because gypsies fascinated me! Perhaps it was because, like them, I too, was always on the move. I think, deep down, I envied them — how, unlike me, they had found stability in movement. As long as they had their tribe around, they were fine. Gypsies taught me that like love, home was not one place or one person, but a feeling. Sometimes, even just the memory of a feeling, which could manifest in all kinds of ways — in places, food, sights, sounds, smells… Perhaps, that's why Nandurbar didn't feel like home anymore. My peepul felt aloof and the Homeless Peacock/Water Phoenix had disappeared.

After leaving Central India, we regularly shuttled between Bengal and Khandesh. Like vapour fills up an empty space, crowded trains began to slowly fill a vacuum, eventually beginning to feel more home than home. Paper cups of tomato soup with a flavour that only the Indian Railways could cook up, and which I had once found too tangy, gradually turned into the taste of home. Vegetable cutlets lost their insipidity, suddenly transforming into nuggets of familiar deliciousness. But what I loved most was the Railways' version of egg curry and rice served in compartmentalized steel thalis. The two eggs would jiggle and dance to the rhythm of the speeding locomotive, and downing them without spilling or making a mess was an art I was proud to have mastered over time. Being a Railway Kid meant that I was also lucky enough to travel with Pup-Pa to pantry cars to see how these goodies were cooked up. Anybody else might have been horrified at the apparent lack of hygiene on Indian trains. My desperate self though, quickly banished the thought. I brainwashed myself into thinking lovingly of the Comfort Food Menu served up by Indian Railways as being the best. I never once fell sick eating train food — and I was a regular traveller.

Comfort Food is not necessarily your mother's cooking, but tastes of the familiar. The Taste of Safety like the

Smell of Relief. M's curry with minced paneer dumplings that Devil No. 1 generously helped himself to before they were ready for guests, the coconut sweets she made on festive occasions, the steaming rice she ladled out of her pockmarked *haandi*, serving it with mashed potatoes, onions and boiled egg in ghee — which she made regularly — was nirvana to the devils. The cook, the foods and their tastes were perfectly normal to the devils, yet to me, they were the Tastes of Terror, terror so strong that it took decades to break it.

One mother's cooking is not necessarily Comfort Food for another's child. Did this also mean that one child's mother might not be another child's mother even if she loved the child just as a real mother did her own?

I loved working out such earth-shattering theories. Each had the potential to change the world but before an answer could present itself, I would fall asleep, lulled by the rural scenery and sight of green fields and sometimes barren lands, rivers, bridges, forests, villages and hills that would swish past my train window.

My theorizing brain's favourite subject was 'Mothers'. I don't know who had bestowed the title of *Maahaara Mein* (the motherless girl) on me. It was usually used to refer to me in the second person, often in my presence, and almost always by mothers, bringing with it exaggerated displays of pity and affection in plenty. Most times, it was almost impossible to distinguish between the two. All was forgiven to this *Maahaara Mein*. She could do no wrong. I caught on to this quite early and exploited this to its full advantage! With it, I gathered a constant supply of books, Gems, Dairy Milks, *kaalo lojens* — lozenges typically available in Calcutta that were so dark purple that they appeared almost black, and that magically tasted sweet, sour and spicy all at once — even as my older cousins looked on furiously; a kind of fury for which they were made to feel guilty and asked to be kinder. I was *Maahaara* and they were not.

In the two-storeyed Ancestral House in Calcutta, the eccentric UndiagnosedAutisticUncle lived upstairs with his family and the insanely loving aunt who had once come to visit the devils. When P and M came to visit, they lived downstairs with her family, which included a rose-ringed parakeet who squawked incessantly whenever he saw me. No matter which floor I ate on, though it was mostly downstairs, every meal was a treat. *Loochi* and potatoes in a spicy gravy or triangular *porontha* for breakfast. Potatoes in *posto* — cooked poppy seed paste — and Bengali french fries. Tons and tons of tiny prawns called *chingri* were snuck in generous quantities onto my plate and into vegetable dishes by aunts all around me who would coax me into eating them. Then, there was *shompapdi* and *payesh* for dessert.

Almost always, I ate downstairs because that's where the most loving mother figure I had ever known, lived. She was like the mother goddess. I called this tiny aunty Big Mother. Simply sitting beside her, bathed in the fragrance of the incense she burned at the altar as a part of the endless rituals she performed for the dozen or so gods who lived there, was magical. I felt the terror, the Tentacle, leaving me free to experience the Smell of Relief. It lifted the opaque jet black shadow that had descended onto me and I could feel peace permeating my slender form, just as I had felt peace by my peepul, a peace that I had almost forgotten.

Many aunts showered me with love, but it was her whom I followed everywhere like a lovesick puppy. She, on her part, drenched me like she drenched whomsoever she met with unconditional love. She had that in abundance within her — more than any other human I had ever met.

During the traditional afternoon siesta time, the entire city slumbered. Big Mother slept next to me, patting my back gently until my demons couldn't help surrendering and then melting away under her love, until I fell into deep, nourishing sleep. She took me to the market and into her world. Big Mother introduced me to the sweet shop vendor who smilingly asked me what my favourite dessert was and gave me *shompapdi* and *kaalo jam*; the tailor gave me colourful buttons to collect and play with; the fishmonger threw in *chingri* as tiny as Gems, saying they were for me.

Then, there were the neighbourhood women she bumped into on the street, who, like her, had stepped out for errands. They patted my hair and pulled my cheeks. They asked me questions and gave me sweets. I was back in Eden, a different sort of Eden, but Eden, nevertheless. I stopped hiding behind doors. My heart murmured less and sang more. Freedom returned slowly to my feet, which stopped freezing solid and instead melted into a series of hops, skips and dances. Nightmares left. Childhood returned.

Over the next few years, there was a gaggle of aunties who mothered me. Big Mother remained my most beloved, though, so beloved that on the journey back to Nandurbar, I almost ran away from the train (with a small bag of books, a toothbrush, paper soap and a few clothes, all that I thought I'd have needed) as it crawled out of Howrah, but then it picked up speed. Dizzy from staring at the hypnotic tracks, I lost my courage to jump off. And then of course, as the train went deeper into that stretch of the country, I remembered that if there was Big Mother in the east, there was Manga Kaka's unconditional love waiting for me in the west.

I like to believe I raised myself. But it was these pieces of motherhood that raised me, most of all Big Mother and Manga Kaka. But there were others too, Nimba Kaka, Ramdas Kaka, Digambar Kaka, Suman Kaka, Kisan Kaka, the brothers Rana Pratap Kaka and Kana Pratap Kaka...who, like Manga Kaka, were somehow, a part of Pup-Pa's job. Often, I ate at their homes. Simple, spicy Khandeshi *bhaaji*s. Dusty *bhakris* bursting with the flavours of their difficult lives. Occasional treats like *pooran polis*. *Kombadi* (chicken) curry. But mostly, quick snacks or breakfasts of tapioca *khichdi* with peanuts. Sometimes, I ate out of their tiffins. The first time I ate Kisan Kaka's smooth Gujarati rotis was also the first time I learnt that rotis could be made out of rice! I sometimes shared Rana Pratap Kaka's basic lunch of *jawaar* rotis, as strong, sturdy and thick as himself. He ate the rotis simply with onions or pickle. Thus, I toured the country's many untold stories.

In these foods of the more modest, I found the greatest luxury, the luxury of Comfort. When they toured their *muluk*, their villages, or went on pilgrimage to Pushkar, Kumbh Mela or Shirdi, they returned with myriads of sweet and savoury homemade treats — *chaklis*, sweet, thin crispy plates of sesame seed and jaggery and other treats that remained nameless.

Like a river in spate, this loving mismatch of foods washed over me, sweeping away my trauma and terror, making me forget that a Tentacle still lived inside me.

The Taste of Relief flooded over me.

Somewhere in these train journeys between the country's east and west, more aunties began auditioning for a role nobody bothered to tell me about: that of a second mother to me. There was no shortage of applicants. Pup-Pa had a secure government job, a big bungalow full of servants, an easy child who preferred to live in books. So, it wasn't surprising at all that Pup-Pa had what I can only describe as an informal *swayamvar* — random women I had never seen before queued up as if for a job interview, smiling at me, calling me *Mona*, *Mamuni*, *Shonamuni*, anything but my name! Old enough to know that such nicknames are generally reserved for familiar young ones, not strangers, I found such fakeness repulsive. My ego, which was several inches taller than me, was naturally insulted.

The circus finally ended in a wedding downstairs that I did not attend. This was fine, more than fine, because I was upstairs in the Ancestral House eating chow mein and nursing Kaalu — a black, muscular stray dog with white patches on his hind legs. He had appeared that afternoon with his buddy Laalu, another big, muscular stray who might as well have been his twin only that his colours were rust and white.

Wherever Kaalu walked, his left foreleg left a tiny stream of blood. Instinctively, I knew that I had to give him first aid. Motherhood had manifested in me for the very first time, out of the blue, taking me completely by surprise. But this was no time to add to my existing theories of motherhood. Kaalu's wound showed no signs of clotting as I led him around the street. Despite his injury, he happily followed me to the back of the house where the staircase went up to the second storey. I grabbed his forelegs and dragged his weight across the two flights of stairs until we were upstairs, hind legs, human legs, tail and all. Kaalu cooperated fully with the whims of a child half his size, not once protesting this mighty discomfort of being dragged upstairs by his forelegs.

In the bathroom, I filled up a tiny basin of water and poured into it half the contents of a bottle of Dettol. Satisfied, I gently immersed Kaalu's paw into this healing brew, certain his paw was now properly disinfected. Grabbing a bandage, Soframycin cream, scissors and tape, I dressed his wounds with tender loving care, certain that any Red Cross nurse would have been proud of me and would have taken me to a war zone to help. I cleaned up, dragged him to the corner room, and held him in my tiny lap as I read him some fairy tales. Kaalu was anything but a villain, but he agreed that he did look a lot like the picture of the big bad wolf in the book. My therapy was working, and he looked a lot better already. We were partially reading, lost in a faraway, fairy-tale land, when we were interrupted by someone especially sent up to keep me company and to avoid 'scenes' that I could have potentially created. The messenger came bearing my favourite street and Comfort Food — chicken chow mein.

Nobody had remembered to tell me that there was going to be a wedding — let alone my own father's wedding.

But then, what else can be expected from grown-ups? They are always so anxious, so afraid, and so insecure. But of course, I knew. I knew in the way children always know everything. Of course, I lapped up the bribe, but there had been No Knead. I had just saved Kaalu's life and I couldn't have been happier or cared less.

The woman who had fit the job description of a new bride for Pup-Pa — of playing with me — turned out to be the exact polar opposite of what the books had taught me about wicked stepmothers. Far from being evil, she was elegant, beautiful and sweet. She had a silent, royal grace that I had not seen in anybody except for Thamma, who was actually blue-blooded and hailed from a zamindar family in present-day Bangladesh. Even to my child's eye, she appeared much, much younger than Pup-Pa. She seemed calm, secure, not needing to prove herself, not needing to call me nicknames to establish familiar affection. Instead, she offered me a red and yellow packet of chips that I had never seen before, incidentally called Aristocrat, together with a small pack of Pickwick wafers. With these offerings, she invited me gently to play with her. There was this purity, this innocence about her, which would have made it so easy to take advantage of her, but it was because of exactly this quality within her that I did not want to trouble her, not even in jest.

We became Fast Friends. Her presence in my life also posed a dilemma. If I were to call my latest mother figure, 'Ma', then what would I call Maa by, I asked Pup-Pa.

'I have Maa, even if she is dead. If I am to call my new mother Ma, then what would I call Maa?'

'Call her Ma,' he replied instantly.

Grown-ups love planning and being prepared for anything and everything. Clearly, he had been expecting this question to pop up and had already rehearsed the answer in detail.

'She is giving up her entire world in the big city and moving to Nandurbar for you, so it would be mean if you didn't call her Ma,' he explained. I stared at him. 'You can call your Ma, Amaar Maa (my mother),' he said, putting the matter to rest.

Mother No.1 had two *a*s. Mother No.2 had one *a*. And with this simple twist, the mothers in my life settled into their newfound names, fitting as perfectly as pieces of a jigsaw puzzle. An ease that I envied as a growing misfit, a Complan girl misfit, who would try her whole life to fit in, in vain.

The days were pleasant. I returned to a school where I had studied briefly and where Mother No. 1 had taught science to high school students. I threw a tantrum once, something my stepmother did not stop me from doing. Years later, I'd realize that I had done this because I wanted to cling to my original memories of school (kindergarten) with Amaar Maa. Mother No. 2 let me wear my chocolate brown overall skirt that had been my kindergarten uniform instead of the deep V-neck pinafore for first graders and up. Finding no audience for my rebellion, I gave up and donned the appropriate uniform after a few days.

Amaar Maa had never allowed me to eat at the snack vendor's stall next to the school, preferring to feed me puffed rice balls glued together with melted jaggery. But my new Ma was much younger and less traditional. She bought me *kachoris* and samosas from this guy, inculcating in me a lifelong love for tamarind chutney. After I had rested, she would wake me up and gently make me solve notebooks full of question papers that she had painstakingly made for me. Naturally, I topped the class that year. I also won my first certificates in speech and poetry competitions.

Ma worked patiently with me, not once losing her temper until I aced my multiplication tables. She got me a big black and golden hexagonal Ajanta clock and taught me to tell the Time. This new knowledge caused great upheaval in my life. It turned Time, which until now had been my servant, into my master. Sometimes, she let me wear her beautiful white and blue HMT bracelet watch. She introduced me to spicy street food, to Aamir Khan, to her favourite movies, *Qayamat se Qayamat Tak* and *Maine Pyar Kiya*, from her college years in South Calcutta. She told me about hip and happening South Calcutta. She let go of my long, tall frocks and dresses and introduced me to denim and to miniskirts too. It felt incredibly cool to be with her. She was so classy.

It was the most normal and most stable year of my childhood yet. It was refreshing to be just another kid whose life revolved only around school, studies, play and unconditional love. I finally got what all the hype was about. Having a real mother, finally, was absolutely magical!

One afternoon, one of Pup-Pa's many Railway friends, Gandhi Uncle from a town called Gandhidham, whom I called GandhiGandhidham Uncle, visited. He fussed over me as anyone would over any small child they knew and made me sit in his lap and listened intently to my tall tales and endless chatter. Much to my delight, he gave me a Five Star. Pup-Pa was out and Ma had stepped inside to bring him some tea. He pressed my chubby arms so hard that they hurt. One arm had trapped my arm, crushing me painfully to his chest, while his other arm had tightly trapped my thigh.

Inside me, the Tentacle suddenly grew tall, reminding me that I was being held captive as he planted a porcupine kiss on my right cheek — a kiss so prickly that my dimpled baby fat hurt all over. I shuddered, I grimaced. That strange and disgustingly familiar hardness in his lap confirmed the Tentacle's message. My body froze. My eyes looked into GandhiGandhidham Uncle's eyes like a trapped animal looking into the hypnotic eyes of its predator. His face had changed, as had his attitude. *He* had changed. Changed into something I recognized so well. My mouth opened, but my voice, now so used to living in Eden, was in such deep shock that it didn't produce a single sound, not even a whimper. My past life had returned to ensnare me.

'What's going on?'

'Manga, Nimba, where are you? Is this how we treat *Sa'ab's* friend?'

Ma had appeared out of nowhere and was staring at GandhiGandhidham Uncle in the eye, pulling me out of his clutches and into her arms, as if it were the most natural thing to do. 'You, little Miss, it is time for your nap!' she said, as she gently carried me into the other room. This was unusual, as we both knew that unless I was at Big Mother's, I never napped during the day.

Shaking uncontrollably like a deer, I burst into tears. Perhaps the sudden quiet had warned her, even if it had been only for a few seconds. She said nothing, just held me close. It was the first time a grown-up had saved me. It was the first time I realized how only a girl could understand what another girl was going through and save her. After a long time, when I pulled away from her, I noticed a tiny puddle on the floor, the dampness of my frock and her saree. I had wet myself — and her — in my fright.

When we returned, the room was quiet. The cup of tea and the biscuits lay untouched. There was no sign of GandhiGandhidham Uncle. Perhaps he was mortified at what he had done. Perhaps, he had killed himself. I don't know and I never saw him again. Thank God!

6

In the Bardo

My crisis with mothers — and the lack of them — was over, but my insecurities still did not go away. Ma was my best friend, my protector, my teacher, my cheerleader, my guardian angel. I loved her like I had never loved before. Having lived in both Eden and in Hell, I had now learned that:

1) Heaven never lasted.
2) Hell was always around the corner.

My fears manifested soon enough. Eden was soon broken. One day, Ma left with no notice whatsoever, ironically quite like Amaar Ma. She did not leave on a raft, amidst pomp and show. She left unceremoniously, holding through the bars of a train window, the outstretched fingers of my small self, perched as high as my toes would let me. My tears wetted the rails, her arm, my hand, the platform, our lives, silently ruining everything.

Years later, I was able to put together bits and pieces that MultipleSources had told me. Somehow, I had always known that this would happen — that she would eventually leave to have her own child. A child whom she would love more — much, much more than she had ever loved me. Right now, the immediate cause of her going away was the growing rift between her and Pup-Pa. A petty misunderstanding had birthed this separation, the grown-ups said. And as usual, nobody had the courage or the incentive to explain this to the two of them. So, she had decided to live in Calcutta. What could be more nourishing than returning to the familiar warmth and comfort of the city she had always lived in, the only place she felt she belonged. Who knew about Comfort better than me!

And so, train journeys covering the long expanse between the east and the west of India resumed again, slowly at first, much like the giant metal wheels of the trains themselves that were carrying us, as their engines sluggishly woke up to life. I was getting tired of these patterns — of these cycles of abuse, love, train journeys, mother figures, predators... The truth that nobody wants to face is that childhood is imprisonment, where freedom is doled out in penurious quantities, quite by chance. A child is fragile, learning to navigate life on Earth, trusting and completely at the mercy of the adults who decide their lives and who, even if they happen to be kind, themselves have no idea about what they are doing, what is to be done and so, are naturally not worthy of trust.

Meanwhile, Pup-Pa got transferred to the neighbouring state of Gujarat, to a bigger town, Valsad. The town was big enough for the fastest train in India at the time, the Rajdhani, to grace it with a stop! Once again, it was just the two of us — Pup-Pa and me. And, of course, a procession of new *kakas* and aunties. The older ones had passed on the baton of motherhood to the new ones in a strange, invisible relay race.

Pup-Pa formed a committee that held Valsad's first Durga Puja, a tradition that continues till today. The number of Bengalis in the city grew. They were genuinely nice. But life was not. Like an industrious earthworm that knew it could get crushed anytime while it went about the business of existing, I too kept vigil so as to not fall prey or be crushed by random predators, all the while busy with school, studies, books, birthday parties and *pujo* performances.

The mother goddess, with her children, moved her dancer eyes from side to side in approval. Nobody believed me of course, when I told them this. Nobody, except for the children, all of whom Pup-Pa loved more than me. He never hit them, and just like their parents loved me more than their own children, they never hit me, either. Why were parents always nicer to other children? Why were they always more free with them, more generous with presents of chocolates and candy, and certainly with their attention? Years later, I'd discover that I had been wrong all along, that this simply wasn't true. These were just other performances grown-ups would put up unconsciously, without realizing what impact their actions might have on children.

Pup-Pa's constant travels across the country to participate in protests for the rights of railway workers meant that my education began to suffer — seriously. It didn't matter that unlike other children, I was fluent in concepts like *morcha*, *julum*, Pay Commission, and *mazdoor ki maang*. I was also well-versed in slogans, songs and rhymes, which still had Time as their servant:

1) *Amaar Naam, Tomar Naam Vietnam.*
2) *Amaar Bari, Tomaar Bari Naxalbari.*
3) *Inquilab Zindabaad!*
4) *Har zor julum ki takkar mein*
   Sangharsh hamara nara hain
   Jo na mili mazdoor ki maang
   Rail ka chakka hoga jaam.

I took my first-term examinations in one school, and my second-term examinations in another. I went to second grade in one school and without taking the final exams for that grade, I aced my admission tests and skipped straight to third grade in the next school. Eventually, I became a privileged third-grader who travelled to another city, a one-hour train ride away, in addition to a 20-minute bicycle ride on Ishwar Kaka's bicycle to attend the best school in the region. I'd be ready in the wee hours, smelling of Lifebuoy and BoroPlus with Pup-Pa putting paper pins to hold my golden retriever-coloured cloth belt to the pinafore of my school uniform.

He had ordered a huge bunch of four-lined notebooks and painstakingly covered them in plastic-lined light brown paper and stuck colourful name labels of my choice, only to discover that this school prescribed single-lined notebooks. So, we had to dispose of the whole bunch. He missed dates for school meetings and would often miss other dates like Sports Day and Annual Day. Daily tasks, so simply, effortlessly and meticulously executed by women and homemakers — like Big Mother and Ma — could barely be tackled by men like Pup-Pa, who otherwise could stand on stage delivering highly charged speeches that held hundreds captive.

And so off I went to my new school, commuting daily on the Flying Ranee, first with the wrong and then with the right set of notebooks firmly tucked into my schoolbag. My co-travellers were all manners of office commuters. It was a strange train suffering from some sort of an identity crisis. Unlike Indian trains in those days, and like the many London and Bombay double-decker buses, the Flying Ranee too was double-deckered with a chair-car interior. Decades later, I'd board similar trains in California and write articles in them as I sometimes wrote homework on this one. Perhaps the Flying Ranee was a pioneer of future rail travel in India. True to its name, it speedily and efficiently took me daily to a grand school in the industrial city of Vapi. On board the Ranee, I made many grown-up friends, all daily commuters like me who entertained my childish prattle with great interest, often, far more than the sensible conversations of their co-passengers. Another perk of being an automatically cute child.

With cups of Indian Railways' tomato soup which I always had heavily peppered, I knew I was safe. My days at school were quite unremarkable. After school, I rested on the big sofa in Pup-Pa's cabin, read *Alice in Wonderland* 64 times and went exploring in Pup-Pa's big railway office until evening came and it was time to take the Evening Train (once again filled with the same office commuters) back home, mostly with my father or with a series of *kakas*.

Decades later, I'd realize that these solitary hours were actually hours of neglect by the busy parent. But whatever they were, they were never boring. On quieter days, I ensured that the productivity of the people in Pup-Pa's office stayed minimal as I engaged his colleagues in endless chatter. On still other days, I managed to mortify them. Like once when I was looking for random treasures in the office, I somehow managed to pull on a door and out spilled the contents of a huge carton of Nirodh (government condoms) which the ministry had sent to be distributed to the labourers. At another time, I had pestered a carpenter. Petrified of upsetting the *sa'ab*'s daughter, he had let me shave some wood and then collect enough sawdust—treasure which I had, then unknown to him, saved in the crevices of the motor trolley for safe keeping. An unforeseen side effect was that the trolley mysteriously stopped running, leaving everyone baffled. By the time the problem was diagnosed and fixed, with the culprit being obvious to all, precious time had been wasted and the whole exercise had to be rescheduled.

Engineers like Pup-Pa and a bunch of trolley men (named so by the British for their job of pushing motorless trolleys till they gained enough traction, at which point the nimble trolley men would jump on to the trolley to join the others) would set off routinely, often accompanied by yours truly to inspect if the tracks were in order for trains to run safely. I never felt the need to go to an amusement park — not after such thrilling rides when we went over rivers and hills with the refreshing breeze sweeping across our hot, tired faces.

One afternoon, I managed to build a tower of stones — tiny to all eyes except mine, which saw in them the power of a wall to stop a train in its tracks. All of a sudden, a loud, lusty horn burst through, the kind that belonged to Huge Speeding Express Trains. Oh my God! I had to act fast. I did the best I could, grabbing a red flag to stop the beast and save the many lives it carried. The Huge Speeding Express Train slammed on its breaks, screeching itself to a halt as soon as its driver saw the red flag. Friction birthed bouncing sparks on the metal tracks. My hands went over my ears as armour against the shrill grinding noise of the brakes. Someone saw me in the nick of time and snatched the red flag out of my hand. Startled, I looked up. The *kaka* held a green flag in his other hand and waved it as aggressively as he could.

The Huge Speeding Express Train stepped off the brakes and took off again, with a very angry driver shooting expressions of disgust mixed with disbelief through the engine window.

To the Office People's great fortune and to my misfortune, these dramatic afternoons ended all too abruptly as Pup-Pa managed to get himself transferred to Vapi. This meant a goodbye to my long rides on the Flying Ranee, leaving me with only the second part of my commute on the bicycle. I now spent the afternoons in a neighbourhood full of nice older kids who took me firmly under their wing.

Together, we organized birthday parties for the many strays we had adopted and who lived under our porches as they pleased. Nobody knew who had given them their very strange religious names — Ram Jharogi, Ram Pyaari, Ram

Dulaari, Ram Laadli and so on. And so, they lived under our porches till a chubby puppy, the colour of sawdust, wandered into my front yard. I tied bows with red ribbons on her neck, legs and tail and immediately claimed her as my own. I named her Lucy and declared that her birthday would be on Christmas. A girl suggested we call her Ram Lucy to match the other strays. Luckily, everyone saw at once what a terrible idea this was and vetoed her suggestion unanimously. We collected *chanda* from not just the neighbours but even from everybody in Pup-Pa's office. Office People quickly gave me whatever they could, happy to get rid of me as soon as possible. I even emotionally blackmailed the food stall guy at the station to part with some notes for an orphan puppy's birthday. The puppy was in my arms, so most people could not resist my pleas.

For Lucy's birthday, we managed to procure nine muffins studded with tooti frooti. I bathed her with Lifebuoy soap, then powdered her with Cinthol. Finally, she had fresh red ribbons tied on her and she was ready for her party. All of us helped her blow out the single candle. But only I had the honour of helping her cut into the muffins that we had arranged like pieces of a puzzle to give the illusion of a big cake. She wasn't interested in more than a nibble, so we gladly helped her finish her delicious birthday cake all by ourselves.

Life was fun. Instead of the Tentacle, I now had a real puppy. Before I knew it, I had dropped my guard.

Then, an eventful day happened at school. I was late for the Games Period. The sports teacher, whom I had never seen before, was teaching us to catch a football, which reminded me of the devils. To my disbelief, the ball took on menacing hues and I began to feel scared of it. Scared of a ball! My eyes kept shutting, unable to bear the sight of the football. Is it any wonder then that I kept missing the ball? My classmates stared at me as if I were from outer space. I was otherwise a reasonably cool kid, among the class toppers, Etsektera. I was mortified! After a few attempts, the sports teacher (let's call him S Sir) stopped the class, picked me out, and gently told me it was okay. He asked me if I was indeed Bengali. I nodded. He then asked me about my parents and pointed out the other Bengali children he knew and whose parents he knew as well.

Back home, I practised throwing a ball against the wall again and again, for hours, over several days. I tried to keep count but couldn't as the selfish ball stole all of my focus. The number of throws must have matched the number of people Pup-pa addressed his speeches to, which was countless! Almost always, my hands caught the ball comfortably, just as he caught the audience's attention. I did not need a crystal ball to realize that the ball itself was not the problem. My problem was in trusting the random balls that life itself threw at me. I lived in constant distrust of almost everybody and most certainly, of life. There was nothing I could do to hone my ball-catching skills, so I gave up, resigning myself to whatever humiliation lay in store for me. Surprisingly, from then onwards, Games Period switched from ball-related sports to focus on running and other forms of athletics — all of which I was allowed to avoid.

One day, I discovered that Pup-Pa was partying with several uncles, something that happened often enough. They were all merrily drinking Scotch together with generous helpings of Chicken 65 and talking raucously about things that made them roar with laughter. Usually, his mates were mostly Railway People, Office People, Comrades, Railway Contractors and several Bengalis that he had befriended in the city. This time, there was one big difference. One of the partying men was S Sir. How creepy! Pup-Pa never dropped me or picked me up or attended events. How had this teacher managed to trace my father who had never been to the school? It must have meant some hard work and researching on the part of S Sir. The predator alarms in my head buzzed loudly, almost deafening me with their full volume. But then I remembered how kind he had been to me, so kind as to keep me away from any of the big ball-catching sessions with the rest of the class. The predator alarms in my head shut down just as quickly as they had sounded. As I walked away, he noticed that I had seen him.

I was back in the backyard with my current obsession — an illustrated comic book version of my beloved *Alice in Wonderland*, a book that would go on to deeply impact my entire life, but I did not know that then. I was sitting at my usual happy spot by the fragile guava tree, its supernatural bark peeled off endlessly like injured skin revealing its hidden magical properties.

Somebody grabbed me by my boy-cut hair, then turned me around, and pulling me violently, had stuck his disgusting TT — Tentacle Tongue — through the rabbit hole of my mouth, deep down into my throat. I was on the verge of passing out, certain that this octopus kiss would gag me to death. I felt myself tearing into a million fragments that merged with the hundreds of splinters on the bark of my delicate guava tree, things that had no name, no power, no description. Here was peace. Here was rest. I watched the body that was supposed to be me with detachment. A detachment that was better than any freedom I had known in a long time. TT shoved itself out and its owner gently patted my shoulder and face and placed me back on my perch under the guava tree, respectfully returning an object back to its place after use.

With a massive electric jolt, my splintered bark-peel-human fragments reunited themselves back into the body that I had just been observing, losing the detachment and the indescribable freedom it had held only moments ago. Only then did I look up to see the octopus. It was S Sir! He was now smiling sweetly, stroking my hair affectionately before leaving. I shivered in the boiling heat of the day. Unable to peel my eyes off from the now empty scene, I stared, waiting for explanations that never came.

My body told me that what had happened just now was a repeat of the second episode of P. What was different now was that I had actually watched this whole episode as a rank outsider, and then returned to my body, once it was all over. This could only mean that I had left my body. Could such a thing happen? Could such a body be trusted? My defective heart, WholeHeartWithaHole, had promised me a mysterious superpower. Was it this — my ability to become a ghost? And go in and out of my body as if walking through revolving doors? Did this mean that like Alice and Homeless Peacock/Water Phoenix, I too, lived between worlds?

I knew who I was this morning, but I have changed a few times since then.

It had to be my superpower! Because shortly after, my body left my body. Again!

A hand woke me up in the middle of the night. A hand that had the insolence to pull down my orange underwear that had a chipmunk on it, to trespass into and toy with the part I peed from. The shadow it belonged to was unfamiliar because it was that of a stranger, one of the several who stayed in our house en route to other railway stations — on duty or to join a trade union protest. Unless they returned again and again or were talked about, I often never remembered who came and went. And I did not remember who this sadistic, ungrateful one was — not his face, not his name, nothing. There was just the hand I wish I could have cut off and burned.

I realized that I was leaving myself to become the wall, feeling the heaviness of its part oil-based paint and the suffocation of its part whitewash, the claustrophobia of the heat it had absorbed from 60 summers. Eventually, I moved to the ceiling like the many geckos squatting in houses across the country and I watched myself pee into the hand in fright. Even then, the shameless, cruel hand continued doing what it was doing.

You may have noticed I'm not all there by myself.

I don't know when I returned into my body. By the time I woke up in the morning to a dry bed, the strange hand and its owner were gone. Had I dreamed up the whole nightmare? As the sun's rays lit up the room, the light yellow outline of a cloud on the bed sheet as well as on my chipmunk panties and the light stench confirmed that it certainly had not been a dream. And while I had lost a lot already, I had not lost my sanity. Not yet.

I fell deeper and deeper into the rabbit hole of my imagination and into the world of books, choosing them over reality. Addicts choose their own coping mechanisms. I used the precious remainders of my scant and fast depleting trust in life and in humans very cautiously. Apart from Pup-Pa, I trusted children of all ages, all animals I met, save for reptiles, and every single labourer I met, and indeed, I met many.

Often, Pup-Pa had to drop me off at homes of random railway aunties as work took him to inspect railway tracks in other towns. They said cheerful byes to him, their smiles shutting as quickly as the front door on his back. That I was a burden on their dear afternoons, the only time they got some freedom, was written all over their faces. Grateful to know that I was at least safe, I set up home in a corner of their living rooms with my books, travelling to Lilliput, Brobdingnag and Laputa with Gulliver. They were happy to meet a child they didn't at least have to entertain. They would give me a snack and after a brief chat, would recede into the dark coolness of their inner rooms. They didn't realize that the *undhiyu* and *kadhi* and *aamras* they fed me was filed away under the label of Comfort Food deep in my memory. Years later, I'd discover that like truth, *kadhi* changed colours depending on the person cooking it.

One of these aunties would insist on playing the Amitabh Bachchan-starrer *Shahenshah* on her VCR for me every time I visited. Initially I found the movie frightening, but gradually, after multiple watches, I took to it. It was the first time I realized that something could be recorded and replayed countless times. Looking back at my fruitless eight-and-a-half-year-old life, I wondered if it too, was a kind of device playing out recordings of abuse and abandonment, over and over again. I wished to travel to the land of the Houyhnhnms, the talking horses that Gulliver had visited and, like him, I did not wish to return. For, many adults around me, especially the disgustingly sick predators, were like the Yahoos that the author had nailed in his book.

Obviously, this kind of makeshift childcare could not remain permanent, especially for a Pup-Pa who had to travel constantly, take on night shifts and be prepared to be transferred to any part of western India. Ever since Ma had left for Calcutta, I had this recurring feeling, a two-part wave of clairvoyance, that went largely unrecognized.

1. a) That I was living in some sort of a world in-between worlds, a bardo.

   Like the Cheshire Cat. Like the Homeless Peacock/ Water Phoenix. No wonder I felt like a ghost.

   I am not crazy. My reality is just different from yours.

1. b) No matter the terrors or the relief, there would be some sort of resolution soon.

During this time, a beautiful dream crept up upon me like silent smoke filling up an empty room. It began to visit more and more regularly, till it became as familiar as one of my fingers. A bird's-eye view of a gorgeous lush green hillock, parts of which were hidden, playing peekaboo with the clouds. Here and there, amidst the unbelievable greens of the trees, were hundreds of thousands of pages floating in space with the mist. A little lake with glassy water reflected the clouds, the lush forest all around and the little sheets of paper. I could not see myself anywhere. Yet, I knew I was there. I was the mist. I was the pages. I was the forest. I was the water mirror. I was nothing. I was everything.

7

Up the Ridge

Words like 'boarding, boarding school, residential school, dormitory, girls' hostel' and 'hill station school' began to pop up regularly in the innumerable grown-up conversations I eavesdropped on as diligent preparation for a possible future career in espionage. The string of synonyms was to me what a daily horoscope in the newspaper was to a sceptic. Still, this army of synonyms walked into my reality with uncanny astrological accuracy. There were more train trips and more admission tests, all with the nonchalance of routine. I complied, preparing for and taking admission tests at private schools, passing most but not joining because Pup-Pa, a government servant, couldn't pay the unwritten, mandatory requirement usually mentioned in hush-hush tones — the minimum 'donation'.

All of it was an adventure. Thanks to my tormentors, I had learned to live every breath to the fullest. Barring a few horrible incidents, every hour I spent outside the scary kingdom of P and his devils was freedom (even if it was under the Tentacle's shadow).

But Pup-Pa was tired of running around in circles. Finally, he settled on a government boarding school where no hush-hush voices asked for that mandatory donation. We boarded the fanciest normal train in India, the Rajdhani, and went to Delhi for the national admission test for the best boarding school the Railways had in Mussoorie. I excelled in all the subjects but left most of the Hindi paper blank. While I was fluent in the language, I could barely read or write in it — and who could blame me? I had lived in my own experience of attending eight schools across the country, and it wasn't taught in the lower grades back then, apart from in northern India. I failed the test, the first time I failed in anything. It was the start of a trend — failure in academia, failure to get a job, failure to be cool, failure to have good friends, failure to thrive — a set of failures that would end only when I reached my 20s.

The railway world we lived in was chock-a-block with trains and an endless stream of kind uncles and comrades. Barring the anonymous Hand that had made me don dark-coloured lenses of suspicion to filter everybody and everything, everyone else had been mostly very warm, genuinely kind and loving. One of these uncles stood out for he had a moustache just like Hitler or Charlie Chaplin. I couldn't decide which, but it was balanced by his kind, disarming eyes. He told Pup-Pa of his daughters who had graduated from a boarding school in the hills near where he lived, from a school run by compassionate nuns with maternal instincts. This snippet from a casual conversation changed my life. Pup-Pa did all the finding out, and yet another train ride followed, with yet another admission test…

By now, these endless railroad journeys and examinations had blurred into a well-blended smoothie in my memory, rendering the ingredients unrecognizable. All I remember is riding up a rocky mountain road in a jeep taxi, a road that had trees hanging treacherously on one side, as if waiting to kiss and then fall unsuspectingly on a passing vehicle and smash it and its contents, people, luggage and all... Frightened, I looked at the weather-beaten road, which looked like it could crack anytime, making us freefall into the tranquil, deep canyon alongside.

Important Lesson No. 4: Extremely rugged beauty can be extremely frightening.

I was groggy when we landed finally at the Holiday Home — a pretty little railway guest house with a corridor full of rooms on either side, just like hotels with cheap marble flooring and home-cooked meals. I'd soon discover that its menu had nothing from my Comfort Food Menu. Holiday Home was so central that we could walk from there to everywhere in the little town. We hiked in the nearby woods past what sparked a memory of a fairy-tale lake. A lake scooped out with fingernails. Here was living proof on the usefulness of fingernails as opposed to cutting them. Pup-Pa ignored my wisdom.

We went on a pony ride that introduced me to one of those things that grown-ups always complained about — backaches. We walked to a nearby place that sold all kinds of cool clothes and trinkets, called Tibetan Market, but when I asked the shopkeepers, none of them said they were from Tibet. They were all from Nepal! Finally, the school presented itself into view.

What was most special about Holiday Home was its sweet and very intelligent attendants. They understood my many philosophies about mothers and foods and agreed that their home-cooked meals didn't quite make the cut. Even more cool was the terrace of the Holiday Home, which had a spacious, round bamboo-stick hut that one could access at any time, complete with a sloped, round bamboo ceiling. Luckily, there were no pandas around. Inside was a TV, a table and plenty of sofas. I had never seen a house on a rooftop before, leave alone one made out of bamboo! I decided that when I grew up, I would have an office just like that so that whenever I stepped out of my cabin, I would have breathtaking green mountains to look at, preferably with pandas, so it had to be an office Made in China, in China.

The next morning, we finally walked up to the school. A metal gate, tall and skinny like strange trees in forests, enclosed an uphill, winding road which disappeared beyond bends and curves, revealing its contents once you walked up the path. I lifted my head to look at the top of the gate, squinting in the harsh sunlight. The school's name looked down at me regally, its capital letters forming a shiny arc. Each letter stood apart from its neighbours, with the result that the nameplate resembled a series of skeletal moulds rather than a finished product. The serpentine road was flanked on either side by twin parapets with steps so long and generous that it was safe to walk on them. On the left of the parapet, a house was being constructed. On the right was a short structure with a small board that declared that the building was the Children of God Hostel.

'Is it full of orphans?' I asked. Didn't children belong to their parents? It's only when they don't have any that they belong to God, Mother Earth, Etsektera.

'Obviously not!' Pup-Pa said as he shot me a stern look.

'A hostel,' he added, sharply.

'One of many.' He pointed to another anonymous house on the left that we had walked past and had somehow missed.

'Anyway, now focus on your test.'

I braced myself for the uphill climb. What might have been a stroll for rugged mountain folk was going to be quite a climb for my nine-year-old self. The more we walked, the more the path revealed itself. Trees, patches of greenery and lovingly tended to pretty gardens lay here and there. A block of short buildings with a playground appeared on the left, then a big garden with flowers, ferns and many other plants. Some plants grew in quirky pots. There was a regular bathroom sink and a big bathtub full of flowers. Right above these were more buildings, a bunch of rocks with a glass cabinet fixed into them. A colourful statue of a thin woman with a kind face stood inside it. To the statue's right was a spiral metal staircase that lay hidden by dense foliage. It was beautiful!

'We go this way,' said Pup-Pa, pointing to the left. I looked down, realizing only then that my feet had already begun taking me automatically to all these beautiful gardens on the right. The left was regular open spaces, more gardens, paved roads and an empty compound, which my stuttering clairvoyance (amateur clairvoyance with an amateur's under-confidence) said (correctly) was for the school assembly. A few feet away lay another much smaller compound with a flight of stairs going down to a cement basketball court below.

Upstairs was the examination hall, a big airy room full of light and a stage hinting at its regular job of being the school auditorium.

I took the test. In the Hindi paper, one of the words I had to make a sentence with was *nakal*. I did not know its meaning, so I asked the supervisor what it meant.

'That would be cheating!' she said as she scowled and walked away, leaving me dumbfounded both at her rudeness plus meanness, a two-in-one. She had given me the meaning of the word in her reply, for *nakal* indeed meant copying or cheating, but I did not know that. I was yet to decipher the mysterious ways of grown-ups. And so, I simply wrote the best response I could think of: *Mujhe nakal shabd ka matlab nahee aata*. I do not know the meaning of the word *nakal*.

The bell rung soon after. I submitted my papers and walked down to Pup-Pa.

'Sorry Pup-Pa. I did my best. But I don't think we will be making it here,' I said tearfully, devastated at having failed him.

'Why, what happened Pup-Pai?' he said, trying to sound more concerned about my state, but he couldn't hide his worry (what if I didn't get through here either!). It was written all over his shadow, leave alone his face. I showed him the question paper. 'I have been studying Hindi. But I did not know the meaning of *nakal*. So, I might fail in Hindi again and we might not make it.'

'That's okay,' he said. 'Let's go!'

'Where?' I asked.

'To Holiday Home. Then, for ice cream,' he said, as he smiled.

The Smell of Relief washed all over me like a waterfall. I sighed, then turned around and walked back to collect my things.

When I returned, Pup-Pa was speaking to a short nun with chubby red cheeks and big round eyes. The laughter in her eyes showed up as a big warm smile. If you looked closely, you could see that it had travelled through her entire body, filling her immediate surroundings with mirth.

'Hello, I am Sister Constance,' she said, extending her hand. I couldn't help staring at it. Joy had incarnated into a person and was extending its hand to me. (Should I take it?)

I was not used to being treated by grown-ups this way, especially by people in authority. I was nervous. Smiling awkwardly, I placed my hand in hers, shaking her hand with the strength of a sheet of paper from one of my notebooks.

'What's your name?'

'Rituparna.'

'Spelit.'

I froze, unable to make sense of what she had just said.

'Spelitchild?'

More foreign words. Was this Latin for *nakal*?

'Spelling!' nudged Pup-Pa with a gentle pat (which meant anxiety, warning, Etsektera) on my shoulder. 'What's the spelling of your name? Sister is asking.' The familiarity of his voice and his touch of many meanings woke me up from this snowballing newness that I was finding hard to digest.

'R I T U P A R N A,' I answered.

'Do you miss your mother?' she asked.

'No,' I answered honestly.

'Really? How come?' Her smile shifted into another one of a different kind.

'I have trees. Stars. And Pup-Pa,' I said.

She smiled a third type of smile.

Important Lesson No. 5: There are many types of happy smiles.

My first Cornetto, my first softie, my first pizza and my first boat ride later, I discovered that my *Maahaara* status and my stellar performance had led to my acceptance not only minus the unofficial, unwritten and mandatory requirement mentioned in hush-hush voices—the donation—but with a discount on the fee, like an informal scholarship, well after the term had begun.

My father was proud of me. Finally, someone was.

8

Hostel Days

Grown-ups around me happily smashed coconuts whenever new beginnings and auspicious occasions were inaugurated. It was a happy sound and I loved it. Happy sounds somehow silenced the Tentacle, loosened its grip over me and dulled its claws. But I wasn't so lucky. Every big episode in my life entailed traversing the girth of our wide country on the Indian Railways. I was like a Railway Princess changing from one railway palanquin into another. Maybe that's why I was always a misfit, mysteriously craving coconut water no matter where I was — on the coast, in the mountains or in the desert. A Coconut Water Craving Railway Princess Misfit.

Amidst many such tomato soup-peppered train journeys, Pup-Pa and I went shopping for boarding school supplies. It was the middle of the school year, which meant seats were full and I could not become a boarder at the school's on-campus boarding facilities. Until a new spot opened up or till the new term, when someone left, whichever was sooner, I'd have to float in and out of another bardo of sorts by lodging at one of the many private children's hostels dotting the rocky little town.

In Valsad, I picked out bed sheets with purple and fuchsia raindrops falling upon a happy pink mommy duck with an inverted umbrella on her head and countless wide-eyed ducklings by her side. The ducklings looked very lost. In Vapi, we picked locally made raincoats which could fit three of me, the perfect space needed for my the perfect space needed for my existence as a tortoise carrying her shell and world — of textbooks and other more important books — stuffed into a chocolate brown Bata school bag. The raincoat had snowmen with umbrellas on their heads. Designers of children's things in Gujarat seemed to be obsessed with cute creatures who were waterproof and yet balanced umbrellas on their heads. In the last stretch of the plains, a sort of base camp for the hill station my boarding school was perched upon, I picked out more bed sheets. This time, the sheets had Dalmatians coloured in dream-like neon that I'd later associate with Andy Warhol. Mama Dalmatian had her litter of pups around her, some perched on her head, others scattered around. Having gathered enough surreal supplies, I decided it was only fair that Pup-Pa pick something for me now. He chose a few sensible striped towels and a few boring and ugly things like the stuff grown-ups use. These were the mysterious items listed as 'monsoon towels'.

After a few stops here and there, we were back in Calcutta where Pup-Pa lovingly chose more ugly things. Nighties in sizes and *baatik* patterns better suited for the aunties I knew than for a schoolgirl. *Salwar* suits (the first time I had them) that nobody criticized for the fear of breaking his heart. All clothing that nobody appreciated except for the polite maid.

In Bombay, we picked up black ankle-length rain boots so spacious that I could harvest rainwater in them to have my own private and clean puddles in which to float paper boats. In Bombay, we also ran a host of other errands, did a ton of bank work, and also picked up an assortment of board games. My favourite was the one with cool geometric shapes made of steel wires, besides comics for me to read. Determined to beat my failure in Hindi in my previous admission test, I was now reading Nagraj and Commando Dhruv comics in Hindi. Oranges were also added to my supplies. I hated them because:

1. Peeling them sprayed a chemical which burned my eyes and which adults, annoying as always, said was good for the eyes.
2. They tasted sour at best, insipid at other times.
3. I was forced to have them because Vitamin C was healthy.

We boarded the big comfortable train to Ahmedabad, then changed to a smaller, narrow gauge train, about 40 per cent smaller than the others, and due to its designers' lack of imagination, it had absolutely no toy train-like features. It had neither an AC nor tomato soup nor egg curry. Heavily disappointed, I made a mental note to point this out to the relevant railway uncles so that they would do a better job on sprucing up this train. Then, I fell into a dreamless sleep until a hand — *a hand*! It always made terror shoot up through me like bile — woke me up. We had arrived.

The uncle who had told us about the school and another smiling uncle with kind eyes greeted us. The first one was the uncle with the Hitler/Charlie Chaplin moustache. The second one was tall and skinny like a tree, and bald.

I waited for him to turn around so I could decide whether he was to be trusted. He was very warm and smiled kindly at me. He put a light arm around my shoulders and asked me how my journey on the small train was.

I froze. His touch was clean, transparent and full of innocent fatherly love. But any touch somehow reminded me of S Sir. It wasn't this uncle's fault and neither was it mine. We went to his house where the sweetest aunty lived with her two daughters. Two steps inside this house was enough to convince me that it was a perfect, safe and loving home, just like the ones I had always dreamed of. One of his daughters was a few years younger than me, while the other was practically a baby. As Pup-Pa slipped out for endless errands, the older one and I played. Her mother kept returning from the other room in the interiors of the house, and every now and then she would give me a huge, kind smile as if to lovingly check if I was okay or not.

The house would be our base camp for the next few days. My investigations confirmed it to be completely safe, perhaps the safest place I had been at since Ma had left. The Tentacle had scalded my insides, reducing my confidence and trust to ashes, replacing it with suspicion. I told Pup-Pa that this uncle made me feel a little uncomfortable and it would be nice if he didn't touch me so much.

This was the first time Pup-Pa had heard of 'an uncomfortable touch' from me. I could see the shock and pain that flashed through his eyes for a second. This uncle, whom I will call Uncle At, would often say that he looked upon me as one of his own daughters, continued to be warm to me, but looked hurt and never touched me ever again. Utterly mortified, I hated myself for saying this to my father. Would I ever be able to discern the predator from the protector? Would I ever be able to distinguish love that was present from abuse that was absent?

The next morning, Pup-Pa and I climbed up serpentine roads in a jeep taxi. It suddenly struck me that a train of child abusers had completely derailed my life. That it had made me live in a prison of judgement, where the walls of protection were so thick and high, that love might not be able to climb in.

I would be living away from Pup-Pa again. It was now time to embrace a new way of life. Again. It was too much for my body to digest. I vomited. For the entire hour that it took to journey up into the mountains, my head was stuck out of the open back of the jeep, gulping the life-giving cool mountain air, as I retched continuously, leaving a trail of my misery on the winding, hypnotic roads.

Pup-Pa woke me up, which is how I knew I had fallen asleep. He looked crestfallen as he touched my damp cheeks. That's how I knew I must have cried myself to sleep. Perhaps this is how life would reveal answers from now on to questions that were never asked.

I looked around. It was my first time in these mountains. There was something strange about the houses and buildings here. In a forest of grey rocks and tall trees, man-made installations stuck out stubbornly like weeds, out of place in the surroundings. Complete misfits. We walked through the gates of one such building called Dimples Hostel. A tall Caucasian lady with tight curls and eyes the same colour as P appeared out of nowhere. She was Mrs Kipling. She wore a grey dress that reached above her knees. It was the first time

I had seen a grown-up in a short dress and heels, leave alone a foreigner speaking English with a perfect Indian accent. Already feeling knocked out from a mix of sleep, dehydration and a series of firsts, I could no longer tell what was real and what wasn't. How could P's grey eyes show up in a woman, that too in one with such a warm smile and a strange accent? Was I dreaming?

'Welcome to Dimples!' she said cheerily. I felt as though I had landed on a neighbouring planet that I had researched thoroughly but was visiting for the first time. I did not quite know what to make of anything. Luckily, I did not have to. She and Pup-Pa sat discussing a lot of things, wrote notes on papers, then exchanged them, Etsektera. She gave me a number — 16. It was far less fun and far more important than a nickname. This '16' was to be my hostel number, my identity for as long as I stayed there.

With a grace I had never seen before, she took us on a tour of the two-storeyed hostel. Downstairs were the offices and parlour for parents, and for other important people, business, Etsektera. Beyond it were the private rooms where Mrs Kipling lived with her family. The basement housed a big room for birthday parties and other festive occasions. The children lived upstairs.

I had never seen so many girls together, out of uniform, running around in one place. By my count, there must have been close to 60! Neither had I seen so many beds lined up together. Several of the girls stood in random short lines here and there, some to get their hair combed and tamed into ponytails and braids, others to have their nails trimmed or to go to the bathroom. Still others awaited their turns at popular games, Etsektera. It seemed chaotic with no scope for private space, but the place seemed warm — and inviting. Nobody looked deliriously happy — because:

1) Was it their birthday? It was not.
2) Had they met their most beloved person? They had not.
3) Had they found treasure? They had not.
4) Were they given chocolate or cake? They were not.

Yet, the children did not look sad either. Nobody hid behind the few doors or under the many beds. I checked.

There were even more children running around on the terrace. The small chaotic dining hall with its open kitchen didn't look particularly appetizing. A series of unremarkable toilets and small bathing rooms of various sizes lined another wall. The largest of the bathing rooms oddly had an old, galvanized bathtub — the first time I had ever seen one outside of a picture book. Apart from its owner, whose sweetness grew by the hour, the cool thing about Dimples Hostel was the small door in the wall by the first flight of stairs. It looked as if Lewis Carroll had put it there. Squeezing my eyes open and shut as Alice might have, I waited to discover what lay behind the door with bated breath. Prepared for storage, ready for Wonderland.

When my eyes and breath were released to finally take in the view, they and I were surprised. Inside the room were 11 beds, fans and perfectly real-sized little people. A big window let in light. This was the coveted room, home to all the Big Girls who, obvious even to me who had just arrived, were the privileged lot and the most powerful.

Instantly, I wanted to be here! Remembering my *Maahaara* status and the many entitlements it would automatically bestow upon me, my puppy eyes asked Mrs Kipling, 'Is my bed here?' She shook her head. 'No, my child. You're upstairs with others of your age.' I did not hide my disappointment. In fact, I ensured my face exaggerated it and my shoulders stooped, looking sufficiently crestfallen.

'Please, Ma'am. You've given me a number which reminds me of the birthday of my late mother. Already, I miss her a lot. Now, every time I see or hear "16", I'll miss her even more! I am going to be very sad here, Ma'am.'

'Oh!' she said, looking concerned.

'Give me a minute,' she said and disappeared.

It had happened twice! First with Uncle At and now with Mrs Kipling. If you asked for help, you got it. I should have asked for help before. I might not have needed to put a *kolera* curse. The Tentacle shrivelled at my delight.

'Alright, Reetoo. I asked Aditi here,' said Mrs Kipling, indicating the big girl who was now accompanying her. She was a teenager with hideously dark spectacles that made it impossible to see what her eyes were saying.

'Hello. Welcome!' she said.

'Aunty, we will have an empty bed here once Rinkle leaves,' she said to Mrs Kipling.

What kind of name was Wrinkle? Why would any parent name their child that? But then why would any parent give their kid such ugly glasses to wear? And why would they bathe them with Lifebuoy which made them smell like a cleaning agent? Parents were useless. They knew nothing. It wasn't their fault. All grown-ups as a rule, were useless. Not all, but mostly.

'...Ritu, I don't know when that will be, but we can try then if you are ready,' Aditi said. I nodded, upset that I had lost myself in philosophizing (again!) and had missed out on what she had just said. But I was too proud to ask her to repeat what she had just said.

'What she means, Reetoo, is that you're still new and though you're a big child, you aren't as big as these girls, yet. So, you need to get used to the place first before you are ready for this place and are able to navigate the stairs here while in a rush on school mornings.'

I nodded. 'Okay!'

I was shown my bed, the loveliest, by the corner window. The girl in the bed next to mine smiled warmly. She seemed nice. After hanging around for a couple of hours, waiting for me to settle in, Pup-Pa hugged me. We both said our first proper, tearful goodbye.

Thus began my first year of living in a community of young women. I knew I was safe at last, safe to simply be and thus, safe to be free. Yet, I felt lost not knowing what the future held. It was my first time in a truly foreign place with strangers. It was also the first time I was away from everything I knew. This is why Pup-Pa's absence would hurt the most.

A zigzagging line of half a dozen eager faces crowded my corner. Looking at them, it dawned on me that like my new mates, I too, would be living in lines for all of my years here. Perhaps I would stand in more lines than even grown-ups stood in while running their endless errands.

As a Railway Princess, even if I had been just a broke, terribly frightened, unsafe, Coconut Water Craving Railway Princess Misfit, but a princess nevertheless, this hurt my pride.

The residents of this new land didn't know how much they were helping me settle in. They were simply there to play with my shiny new toys and my board games from Bombay. I shared all these happily and gratefully with them. They were children and their natural nonchalance and warmth meant that anybody could play with anybody and their toys even if they didn't know them or their names. Children usually have no hidden agenda or insecurities to hide or attack with, and it is unsaid stuff like this that distinguishes children from grown-ups. That's what helped me settle in at the speed of a Rajdhani train.

Some of the girls had exotic names that I had never heard before in the parts of India I had grown up in: Trisha, Chhaya, Maya, Shilpi, Ami, Basanti, Monica. They did not leave or cringe when I unpacked the decidedly uncool stuff Pup-Pa had forgotten in my backpack — steel plates, steel glasses and spoons, all in pairs from our train journeys — to be put away in my suitcase instead. They were normal, not mean like some kids can be. I decided to become friends with them. Within minutes of our friendship, I turned them into characters in my stories where they accompanied me on adventures like Alice.

It was so, so wonderful just to be with other children!

9

The Runaway

The morning was chilly. After all, we were in the mountains. There were no heaters. I was dressed like a caterpillar with several layers of woollens, and yet it felt like everything had been peeled off my back. Freezing, I took a deep puff from my purple pipe. Was I turning into a butterfly? 'Get up!' Startled, I woke up immediately! Tentacle alert! Somebody called Bahadur was doing something weird. He was going from bed to bed, peeling off every child's quilts and blankets, bringing their comforters to the edge of their beds. I had never seen this ever happen before. Land of Firsts. Like Wonderland. I also learnt this was the most effective way of getting anybody, even the most reluctant of school kids, to wake up, to seek the warmth of hot water to wash their faces with and to get ready for school.

I stood in my first line (Line Number 1 in Land of Firsts, first line ever) to brush my teeth. Then another, to use the toilets (Line Number 2 in Land of Firsts, second line ever). Next (Line Number 3 in Land of Firsts, third line ever) to get my hair pulled painfully by a mean matron — the opposite of Mrs Kipling — into ponytails she then secured with two huge red ribbons. Before I knew it, I was in a blue-grey pinafore skirt, a cream-coloured shirt and red tie that made up the school uniform, complete with red socks and elegant black Bata ballerina shoes. I was hungry but the smells in the kitchen made my appetite disappear. Before I knew it, we were packed like noisy chickens in a cage, only happier, into a jeep driven by another foreigner, a relative of Mrs Kipling.

Squeals and chatter filled the short bumpy ride. I was immediately claustrophobic, certain that I would vomit. Another reason to throw up was that I had never felt uglier in my whole life. The thought of being beautiful or not had never crossed my mind before. It was the way in which we were put into assembly lines and made to get dressed that turned this school rush hour into something that sucked out tiny bits of our little souls. Luckily, school arrived within minutes and I was pushed out of the jeep in the middle of the chattering group, dizzy but grateful that I had spared myself and everyone else too, the horrific inconvenience of vomiting (and being vomited upon).

Up the same winding road we went, like a flock of sheep, guided by a collective 'Hurry Upping' (a new term I had picked up from the girls) energy of the herd. Somebody told me to go right, towards the statue in the glass cabinet carved into the rocks. This was the way to the primary section.

But sounds of music and laughter wafted in from the opposite direction, beckoning to me with the power of an aromatic biryani. Instinctively, I turned left. Soon, I was close enough to decipher the tune and immediately after, the lyrics. 'Another Brick in the Wall'. In a school! The oldest girls, the tenth-graders, many of them flashing badges of power that read, Head Girl, Deputy Head Girl, Captain, Etsektera, were dancing with Sister Constance! The principal sang the lyrics just as gustily as the rest of them:

We don't need no education.
We don't need no thought control.
No dark sarcasm, in the classroom.
Teachers leave the kids alone.

How deliciously ironic! I smiled inside, glad to finally be in 'A Good School'. I turned around and returned with hurried steps to where I was supposed to be, in the primary section.

Here was another little compound with girls playing hopscotch. I asked one of them where Class IV B was. She pointed upwards with a show of irritation. I'd discover the reason for this soon enough — I had robbed her of those super precious 30 seconds of free play time before the school bell.

A small line of girls in a rush blocked my way upstairs. A chubby one among them, said, 'You piglet!' to another, shoving her behind and scooting up ahead, panting non-stop. Another small line replaced these girls. And yet another. Not wanting to be called a piglet, I let all the lines pass like trains on a track until I was the last one left. There were just two classrooms upstairs.

The most beautiful and elegant grown-up I had ever seen addressed the boisterous first class with a grace that surpassed even Ma's. I was already in awe of the natural beauty of the campus and then there was this Lovely

Teacher. I almost entered her class when a girl asked me, 'Are you in IV A? I have never seen you before. Get out if you aren't.'

Unaccustomed to such rudeness, tears welled up in my eyes. Lovely Teacher came up to me and spoke in the kindest voice I had ever heard coming out of a teacher. Clearly, I had had only UnLovely Teachers before this.

'What are you looking for?'

'I'm new.'

'I know. I haven't seen you before,' she smiled.

'IV B?'

'That way,' she said, touching my shoulder, gently guiding me to the room next door and walking back to address her class. Lovely Teacher's kindness made me burst into hot, thick tears, like the ones my pet tree had once shed. I wished she were my mother. I wished I had a mother who was a school teacher like Amaar Ma, without the technical glitch of being dead, so she could work in the school I attended. In that gap, in the breadth of a pillar between the two rooms, and in full public view, I felt deeply vulnerable, acutely aware of just how utterly alone I was. And worse, how utterly alone I was going to be in this foreign land where people even looked like foreigners.

'Come on!' said another voice, not as lovely as Lovely Teacher's but warm in its own way. 'You are in mine.' She too, gently pushed my shoulders with her arm guiding me into class IV B.

'I am Amita Ma'am. And that there in IV A is Ragini Ma'am. I must be very lucky to have you,' she said, gently wiping my tears.

I looked up. Amita Ma'am too, looked Caucasian, just like those pretty little dolls with huge grey-green eyes which opened and shut. She had their light skin, but her own generous and voluminous curls.

'Are you from England, too?' I asked.

'No, I am from Patiala!' she laughed. 'But wait, who else is? ... Never mind. Let's get to class. We will have plenty of time to chat later.'

I chose a spot by the window with my old, comforting friends — foliage from a tall tree that overhung into the lovely garden below. My spot was as usual in the first row, assuring that I continued to be a teacher's pet. Behind me, a sea of busy-bee heads decked in red ribbons and hairbands prepared their books and pencils for the day ahead.

The day finally came to an end. Several jeeps, heaped with children, returned to their hostels, including one driven by the same affectionate Caucasian uncle who drove me and the others to our home away from home. 'Call me Uncle Will,' he said to me while dropping us off and waving goodbye.

At bath time, while we stood in line, I saw yet another person who looked Caucasian but whose accent was even more Indian than mine, especially while pronouncing consonants. I wondered if she was a relative of Aunty Dodo — which is what we sometimes called Mrs Kipling. Like me, she was a child resident at the hostel. Like my teacher, she was another little doll with huge grey-green eyes with curls that were somehow different, blonde, very short, very wild, which even her pixie cut could not tame. She was running around completely naked, shocking me until the matron wrapped her up in a towel and sternly asked her to behave herself. When I asked the matron who this girl was, she told me that I should be kinder because this little child was two years younger to me. She also confirmed that the child was no relative of Aunty's. It turned out that she had a bunch of sisters, all of whom looked like her. More foreigners.

Still standing in that queue awaiting my turn for the bathroom, I learnt more about my country than I had while travelling through it geographically. I learnt that there were people who looked 'foreign' but who were perfectly Indian. Some of them were even from the same state that I had grown up in! Then, of course, there were others who looked Indian in every way, yet felt 'foreign' everywhere — thanks to the Tentacles inside of them.

I also had to learn to gulp down completely new tastes, such as beloved Gujarati dishes like *dal dhokli* (wheat flour dumplings cooked in a sweet lentil stew).

I soon discovered the secret why hostel food was rarely desired. It had little to do with the food itself. Because everybody mostly appreciated their own mothers' cooking and because no mothers were cooking for their children here, hostel food tended to be about a job that had to be done. However, hostelers learn early on to perk up their food with pickles, relishes, preserves and other secrets that mothers and grandmothers specially packed for them in little PearlPet jars. You could top off the insipid with jarred love and make everything taste better. You could top up your dal with *sev* or stuff your bread and butter with *chiwda* and make your day feel better. Little tuck boxes with homemade treasures made living away from home more bearable in a way that letters could not.

There were other treats in store like watching Hindi movies. Romances like *Dil Hai Ke Manta Nahin* appeared to make the older girls, with MovieChoosingPowers, especially dreamy-eyed. I walked in and out of most of the movie screenings, preferring the precious few moments of solitude to be on the terrace either alone or curled up with a book. There is a difference between solitude and loneliness. Solitude is joyous, healing and nourishing to your mind and soul. It is a choice one makes. Loneliness is parasitical, a painful emptiness eating you up from the inside. It is rarely a choice.

Occasionally, some bizarre B-grade movies were shown. Like the horror film *Bandh Darwaza* that was screened once on a rainy, sunless evening. It added new words like *neola* — a Dracula-like vampire — to my vocabulary, which was a strange mix of English, Bengali, Hindi, Marathi and Gujarati. One had to be insanely talented to make something this frightening and ugly like the *neola* in the film. Yet I was hypnotized, unable to peel my face away, even while I shielded my eyes to avoid seeing the horrible creature on the screen. The younger girls wailed loudly like troubled cats, adding to the horror film atmosphere. Some of the older ones placed them on their laps and comforted them like mother hens. Dimple Didi sat me on her lap. I felt safe. Nevertheless, *neola* nightmares took over Dimples Hostel for some days.

My education had begun, teaching me my treat preferences. Food won over films.

When Pup-Pa visited, I asked him if I, too, could get an elixir-filled PearlPet or two. This time, the supplies came from Bombay again via the network of railway families. Walia Aunty, the matriarch of an elderly family I had just met, had sent me the perfect gift. I, too, could show off now. I, too, was cool! PearlPet Cool. It didn't matter that nobody cared. I finally had a way of fitting in. Knowing that I detested pickles, the clairvoyant Walia Aunty had sent me something so sweet and delicious that it could have passed off as jam, had it not been so ethnically tangy, sour and spicy, all at once. A girl named Ami said this was a preserve called *murabba*.

I wasn't scoring in the 90s anymore, which would have been absolutely unacceptable when I lived with Pup-Pa. But first the girls and then an important grown-up called Susan Ma'am, one of Mrs Kipling's family members, informed me that I was doing exceptionally well at school. I was ranked fifth in class and I was scoring in the 70s, both supposedly splendid for hostelers because unlike day scholars, hostelers couldn't count on privileges like extra tutorial support, attention and help from parents, and flexible schedules to study as they pleased, Etsektera.

There were other lessons I learned at Dimples Hostel.

1. Children can help build real things together.
   Once, something had to be built at the top of the building, for which a lot of wood had to be ferried upstairs. We stood in a line covering the entire campus. As if playing a game of passing the parcel, we kept passing a few light wooden boards at a time until the entire cargo was passed on.

2. Like children, small words too, can mean multiple things and do double, triple and even quadruple duty!
   Until now, the word 'boil' meant a boiled egg for me. But now, I learnt about a *boiler*, around which our entire existence revolved as residents of a hill station. I also learned about *boils*, which appeared to grow on almost everyone, and I soon got my share of them as well.
   This was excellent education for the writer in me and Important Lesson No. 6.
3. Beauty is fashion and fashion is recyclable.
   I also got my first lesson in fashion. Stylish mothers, especially from the big neighbouring city of Ahmedabad, would visit wearing gorgeous *salwar*-kurtas that were sleeveless in summer and magically grew sleeves in colder months. I asked a friend how her mother was so fashionable, season after season, and she confirmed that her mother often recycled her old clothes in such a way that they had a new look in the next season. She was also great at turning old sarees into skirts, dresses, drapes and bed linen. Little did I know then that I'd grow up to do exactly this.

I was so used to Pup-Pa's Lifebuoy-smelling masculine world of uncles and Gang of Gangmen that this kind of formal education was not just a breath of fresh air, it was life-changing. I was finally beginning to understand what being a girl meant.

In this feminine world of Pond's Dreamflower talcum powder, Nivea, Lux and countless products, I felt safe.

Even if Bahadur peeled off the blanket with a jerk every morning, it was okay because the Hand was not coming to get me. I was safe. Even if there were Caucasian eyes all around me that reminded me of P's eyes, it was alright because P wasn't there and unlike his snot-coloured ones, these eyes were actually beautiful. I was safe. Triggers and reminders remained, and my body had its scars and its memories. But I was safe.

Safe. How I loved this word! It had become my life's mission. It was the happiest word in the English dictionary.

Surrounded by little women, and busy leading the life of a normal child, I should have felt happy. Instead, I slipped into a well of loneliness. One of the loneliest days was my birthday. Pup-Pa came and threw what Dimple Didi described as the biggest birthday party Dimples had ever seen. Yet, it lacked the coziness of other girls' birthdays, whose mothers would ring in celebrations by cooking up their daughters' favourite dishes to share with the entire hostel. Some of the dishes served at these feasts were new tastes for me. I remember eating vegetarian hot dogs served with green chutney and lentil dumplings in yoghurt, better known as *dahi bada* or *dahi bhalle* — depending on whom you asked, hard, homemade gulab jamuns, and chocolate cakes decorated with Gems.

There was a dance party and fancy cake on my birthday. I had two pretty floral silk dresses, one with a red, and the other with a green border; one for the day and one for the evening party. Everyone, except me, seemed to be having a blast. Pictures were being taken. I was asked to pose with my besties. I didn't have any. I had learned though that it was cool and nice to hug your friends especially for photographs. So I held some of the younger kids in the group pictures. I stood out easily in them with my fancy evening dress, and if you looked closer, you could also tell me apart because of my sad eyes. All those unsaid rules of decorum, unsaid rules of what was cool, those unsaid rules of being good — I learned them all, with the stealth of a gecko.

Pup-Pa, Auntie Dodo and others saw this and went:

'Awww!'
'Look how she has found new friends.'
'Look how she's learning to love the younger ones.'
'Just like sisters.'
'Yes. Just like sisters.'

Pup-Pa thought I was happy. Not quite knowing yet who I was, and still learning to echo others' expressions, I thought I was happy too. The matron could be mean, but Aunty Dodo was lovely. Then there was Sadhana, who slept on a bed next to mine. We laughed together doing funny dances, mimicking Charlie Chaplin's moves in our own style. Then there were those various renditions of 'Silent Night' and other carols where we would drop the words and instead sing out the syllables boisterously: *Waaa Waa, Waain Waain, Wee Wee, Woo Woo.*

Pup-Pa disappeared after the cake cutting. A short search for him revealed that he was holed up in the basement having grown-up brown drinks with Uncle Will. It looked like a scene with the uncles, back home.

But I was glad he was here and that he was happy. Everyone at least seemed to be happy. And I was happy that they were happy.

The stars seemed to reserve all of their 100 per cent shining power for the mountains. They did not do that anywhere else. Looking at them, I burst into tears like I had in the corridor between IV A and IV B. The abusers had managed to snatch something from me. I could not tell what it was, but I knew it by its absence. Perhaps it was this constant feeling of being in some sort of a bardo, of living in-between worlds. Of being unable to belong anywhere. Of being unable to find joy even in stars that shone their brightest for a birthday girl.

One sunny afternoon at school, the last period happened to be the games period. We could do whatever the *hack* we wanted. Everybody loved the games period — everybody, except me. Balls — lots of balls — were involved. And I still did not have the balls to catch a ball. In fact, now that I was so much older, I was even more afraid of them than I was back then. I was now even more deeply self-conscious of my disability and the cruel laughter that my failure to catch the balls might produce. I could not even practise and attempt to improve on my own, a luxury I earlier had at home in Vapi. Being a child meant that unlike a grown-up, I was not in control of anything, not even the basic human right of 'controlling' my own private space. (Years later, I'd do an article on Private Space.)

An epiphany struck me like a bolt of lightning, making me gasp. Solitude was deeply nourishing and utterly priceless! To not have somebody around you all the time, what a deeply precious thing, that was. And how utterly ironic it was that in this piercing lack of solitude, where I lived continuously in a vivacious crowd, I had managed to sink into such intense loneliness. I greatly missed my only living parent, the one constant in my whole life of nine years.

So that day during the games period, while I hung out on the huge cement steps, which doubled up as seats, and practised being a wallflower (a skill that would come in so handy in the near future), a new wave of energy engulfed me. It was still 15 minutes until the final bell for release would ring and children would run out, seizing their freedom for the day. I watched myself quietly pull away, get my stuff and rush to the school gate. The *chowkidar* stood at the gate, dressed as always in policeman khaki colours. Was this to confuse us? Or was the uniform to scare us? I never found out. His body seemed to wake up as he stood up straight, suddenly alert when he saw a child rushing towards the gate before the bell had rung.

'Where are you going, Missy?' he said with an air of importance. 'It's still 10 minutes to bell.'

'I know. I know. You're right, *Chowkidarji*. You're absolutely right,' I watched the new energy in me say with conviction. 'I have to go meet my LG. My local guardian is picking me up early today for a doctor's appointment. I really gotta run.'

Was it the confidence in the voice or was it me, hyperventilating, my defective heart, WholeHeartWithaHole coming to the rescue? Was it that non-boarders were not his concern after school hours? Was he in a jolly mood? Was it that it was so close to release time anyway that it barely mattered? I don't know what it was, but he bought my story. He nodded and pointed towards the tiny gate that the big gate held inside it like a mother kangaroo. Walkers could walk through it, one by one. The big gate was opened only for vehicles to drive through.

'Thank you, *Chowkidarji* Sir!'

He beamed at this sudden show of respect that he saw reserved for superiors with college degrees. He nodded and I ran out before he could change his mind. I ran and ran and ran. I ran so I wouldn't hear him. What if he changed his mind and shouted for me to come back? I ran away from the loneliness that the Tentacle had spread through my cells like a virus. I ran and ran and ran... until I was running too fast for my legs and I fell, rolling down the slope, scraping my knees. This new energy that had taken over me made me get up, immediately. I was determined to proceed according to its plan — a plan I didn't know. It made me keep running, despite my painful, bleeding knees.

On the way, I passed Sudha, a junior from Dimples Hostel, who was actually with her LG. I kept running. But she had seen me and refused to unsee what she had just seen. 'Hey! Reetoo!' she screamed. It was difficult to ignore her. 'Where are you going?' she asked. I panted and heard myself repeat my freshly cooked-up story. 'I have to rush to meet my LG' The bell would have rung by now and any minute, the girls would come flooding out of the gates, foiling my plan, a plan I still did not know!

'I have a doctor's appointment. Enjoy! Bye!' I said, as I resumed running, maintaining my pace, not looking back.

My feet soared rhythmically on and off the tarmac without stopping until I had reached Holiday Home.

With my hands on my hips, I finally paused for breath. The divine mountain air, crisp and refreshing like spring water, entered my lungs, bringing with it a flash of recognition. I finally knew what my plan was. The foreign energy and I acted as one.

Pretending I was a mouse, I crept in as quietly as one, invisible and inaudible. No tourists were around. The caretakers were obviously enjoying their siesta. The door to the roof was unlocked. I took off my Bata ballerinas and holding them in my left hand, tiptoed up the stairs all the way up to the solitary bamboo hut. It didn't matter that the TV cable was not working. It didn't matter that there was no electricity. It didn't matter that I was totally parched and longing for coconut water. I was finally at peace here, the peace of my beloved peepul.

The plan was now crystal clear. I would rest here for now. The caretakers could feed me and ferry me to Pup-Pa a little later. I could sell off my small golden earrings that I wore to raise my ticket money. A runaway heroine had done this successfully in one of the movies the girls with MovieChoosingPowers had shown us at the hostel. There was zero doubt in my mind about my plan. Except for the time I had given first aid to Kaalu, I had never felt such confidence before.

I was so happy that I even sat down to do my homework with a smile on my face. It didn't strike me that if I was running away from school, I didn't have to do my homework!

I completed it in no time. Having nothing to do until the caretakers woke up, I loitered around the terrace, looking at the trees, the squirrels, the birds and the occasional vehicles that passed by. The town was still new to me. Its preferred local transport — small stroller-like iron carts bearing children and adults that were pushed by men — and mysterious white-clad people called Brahma Kumaris, fascinated me. My wandering eyes suddenly froze! My body though, obeying the intelligence of the new energy, ducked behind the wall so as to be completely out of sight to anyone passing by on the road. Overtaking an empty iron cart was the jeep that was to have ferried me back to Dimples. Seated in the front, next to Will Uncle was Auntie Dodo, looking around frantically, as if searching for something. Me! They were looking for ME. (Obviously!) That Tattlecock Sudha surely must have told them that she had seen me running!

Noises wafted in from below. The caretakers were finally awake. I had no time to lose. In complete trust, I ran downstairs to them. Unaccustomed to the ways of grown-ups, I mistook their baffled expressions for pleasant surprise at seeing me there. Handing one of them a piece of paper on which I had written down our Vapi house address, I said, 'Here! I need you to help me get home. Please help me book my ticket.' They looked at the paper and then at me without saying a word.

'I'm a Railway kid, you know. So, I am entitled to a Railway Pass. But I can't prove that now because I don't have Pup-Pa or documents with me. So you'll have to help me buy tickets. Here (pointing to my earlobes), I'll sell these and get money. It should be enough to cover the expenses.' One by one, the trio smiled. 'Okay *bete. Ab aap aaram kijiye.*' I was so relieved! Trustingly, I followed their advice of resting and went back upstairs. A jam sandwich and water appeared. For the first time in my life, heavy mountain water tasted more delicious than a jam sandwich.

'Hello there, Reetoo dear!'

I recognized the voice at once. My heart sank. I turned around.

'Are you alright, my child?' Mrs Kipling asked lovingly, with a smile. My *actual* LG, Fernandes Aunty, also a teacher at the school, emerged from behind her and hugged me.

Much to my surprise, nobody scolded me. Nobody yelled at me. And nobody seemed upset. If anything, they appeared relieved, even a little happy. But though they said nothing, their faces gave away their confusion. Like Pup-Pa, they had assumed that I was a perfectly happy child and that I was doing well at school. My teachers liked me and I had friends. There were even pictures to prove it. I had had a great birthday party. I had not given any sign of any suspicious or naughty behaviour.

I rode back in the same jeep as a VIP.

The next day, Pup-Pa showed up.

'You are not happy. Do you want to come back home? We can leave right away!' he said with wet, tearful eyes. Both of us were crying, but for different reasons. There was no need for an answer. The entire hostel knew by now, even its littlest members. It was that obvious. I took a deep breath, finally inhaling the correct answer. By the time I had exhaled, both my answer and I, had changed.

'No Pup-Pa! I don't!' I said confusing both him and myself. 'I don't want to leave.' He didn't understand the real reason why I said 'no'. He probably still doesn't.

I hated to have to choose between these two worlds. At home, I didn't know what uncle or what hand would attack me and when. At the hostel, I was homesick and deeply lonely. However, in this almost completely female world, I was safe. For the first time in my life.

It was the first time I realized just how precious this feeling of having and living in a sisterhood, was. It made sense to stay in this world, even if one felt all alone in it.

'Would you like to come with us?' Sister Agnes, a strict yet incredibly gentle and kind nun asked me. I undermined the casual tone of her question, not realizing that it was one that would change the course of my entire life. We were playing in the shiny, newly renovated playground at the back of the campus, a prettier, open part reserved for the youngest children from kindergarten to the third grade. Being allowed to come here, was for us, a rare treat. Today was even more special because we got to play on the renovated playground, on shiny new installations all painted in lovely shades of sky blue and white. I was finally getting to play in this huge, round-shaped open cage with two generous seats in it facing each other. The entire structure itself swung like a double metal hammock of sorts. But it was more like a see-saw, rather than a traditional swing, and I had never seen anything like it before! (Nor did I ever see anything like it, after.) I closed my eyes. The sun's warmth danced in patches on my face, moving to the rhythms of the see-saw-double hammock-swing.

'Reetoo, Reetoo,' the voices said. 'Sister is calling you.' The voices forced me to return from my blue-and-white metal planet with its dancing sun, to this present one. I opened my eyes, squinting in the blinding light and finding myself moving like a bat towards the cool, dark steps that had a blob of light-blue. As the blob got more and more in focus, it revealed its human authority shape. My gait became less and less bat-like.

'Good afternoon, Sister!'

'Good afternoon, Reetoo!'

Why had Sister Agnes singled me out? Why had she pulled me by the steps near the third standard classrooms to ask such a vague question? It made no sense. But then, grown-ups often did not make any sense, anyway. I longed to return to my seat on the blue-and-white swing, this time with my eyes open, to see how the sky and the clouds moved before the whimsical mountain weather changed its mind, like it did all the time.

'How are you? Are you happy?'

What kind of a riddle was this?

'Yes, Sister!'

Perhaps all she wanted was a Book Review on the new playground.

'Very happy, Sister!' I smiled.

'Would you like to come with us?' she asked again.

A riddle within a riddle! Did she mean whether I wanted to explore someplace else? Perhaps another part of the huge campus? Perhaps there were more shiny new structures elsewhere? It was not that I wasn't curious, but I had the rare characteristic of being able to stay still where I was already happy, instead of seeking out exciting, greener pastures. Perhaps I had inherited it from hippopotamuses, buffaloes and elephants, my most beloved pachyderms who could sit still in water bodies forever unless they were forced to move. Perhaps I had inherited it from my times with the devils and P, knowing now to hold on tight to things that were working out until they didn't and only then move on. The Tentacle filed its nails.

'No, thank you, Sister,' I said smiling and as sweetly and politely as I could. 'I am perfectly happy here.'

A few days later, Pup-Pa again visited with my local guardian and her family.

'Why did you say "no"?'

'Yes, why did you?' asked my local guardian.

'When did I say "no" to what?'

'To Sister Agnes.'

This was strange! Why was this casual piece of conversation so important to the grown-ups? Why were they so obsessed with something so fleeting and mundane?

'Because I was happy in the playground.'

'Huh?'

'She asked me if I was happy. I said I was. I thought she wanted me to come see another place. I was happy.'

'Ah! That explains it!' Pup-Pa smiled.

'My child. She was asking you if you wanted to move into the Boarding. By a stroke of pure luck, a spot had opened up — some child had to leave. Everybody wants to move to the Boarding. Don't you?' my local guardian gently explained.

'I suppose so,' I said unsurely. I had stayed here long enough to know that the school's own boarding was like the platinum membership of a club, something everybody who lived away from their parents aspired for.

'Never mind. We will try next year when the seats open up formally. This was an extremely rare occurrence in the middle of the school year, and you were the first choice.'

The remainder of the year flew by unremarkably, save for one incident. Somebody who looked like a WWE female wrestler slipped and fell mid-sentence, near the boiler. She turned out to be Aunty Dodo's daughter. Investigations revealed that she had slipped on a stray banana peel. This taught me:

1) Important Lesson No. 7: Slipping on banana peels was not a myth!
2) Important Lesson No. 8: One must trash trash.
3) Important Lesson No. 9: Always be aware of one's surroundings — at all times. Looking down is great practice for this.
4) Important Lesson No. 10: Banana peels are WMDs. Use such weapons wisely.

Pup-Pa and I went shopping yet again, this time with the neatly typed list that the nuns gave out to boarders. We already had the coolest linen, raincoats, Etsektera. But we still needed small, important stuff. Obviously, we took a train to Howrah Junction, followed by a cab ride to the Ancestral House in north Calcutta.

A few days later, Santhosh Jethu, one of Pup-Pa's childhood friends, took us to a really cool place I had never heard of before — a 'handloom'. A stick-thin person operated a big wooden structure, pulling and moving things to bring together a host of brightly coloured threads with effortless ease, as if mixing in watercolours to miraculously create a completely new piece of cloth. It was the most beautiful thing I had ever seen! I badgered Pup-Pa for more details. He began a long, complicated speech, from which two words, 'handloom' and 'weaver', sifted into a folder in my memory where I filed things, like banana peels, for future reference. I knew that I'd consider becoming a handloom weaver when I grew up. 'Consider' because clearly it was hard work and I would have to be trained at a 'Handloom College' to do so.

Later that afternoon, the handloom weaver handed us a roll of cloth that he had woven while we watched. It looked like a ribbon made of stiff, starchy cotton. It turned out to magically have 100 labels with my full name on each, all printed in Lifebuoy-red ink of course! Neat rectangles, as tiny as hummingbirds' nests, delicately held my name like eggs. A magical number, 291, accompanied it like a Siamese twin. Instantly, I knew that this number would rule my life for the next decade.

Perhaps Pup-Pa finally realized his overdose of Lifebuoy? Perhaps he realized that he had painted my whole life with Lifebuoy? Perhaps his friends finally told him that I was a lady now and that it was time to stop clouding my preferences with manly nonsense. Perhaps there were fewer options at the small hill station store. As always, I had various theories, but none of them could explain why Pup-Pa chose Margo — a dark green neem soap that produced white suds. I shuddered thinking of P and how he had worked the soap into a stinging lather gate that didn't let me open my eyes. Pup-Pa thought I was reacting to mountain weather. But then, I quickly reminded myself that:

1. It was not the soap's fault.
2. The soap existed before P. There was no need to tarnish it by associating the colour green with P!
3. That this soap, as dark as the secret Tentacle my body carried, was a huge upgrade from Lifebuoy. The soap that made me smell like Railway Running Homes and the railway men in it and reminded me more of cleaning supplies. I should actually be happy and celebrate!

The last argument sealed the deal. I moved on to inspect tins of Nivea, tubes of Colgate — all brands specified in the list. Then there were items that had no brand names specified: toothbrushes and the single tower of Cinthol talcum powder. Finally, two ugly aluminium boxes, one to fill with books during the monsoon season, and another to fill with delicacies to savour at teatime.

PART II

BOARDING SCHOOL

10

Salvation

Visiting the same place again is never the same. Just over a year later, I was here again, in a completely new way, feeling strange and absolutely unaware of what lay in store. Pup-Pa said goodbye. Unlike other parents who had arrived in a fleet of private cars, Pup-Pa had a series of trains to catch. Around me was an ocean of female faces, dotted by the rare male relative. I tried to look brave, as if the presence of so many grown-ups didn't intimidate me. By now, I had become used to the kind and gentle ways of Dimples' owner and of its residents and some of my teachers. How could Boarding be anything but better, then? There's nothing to be afraid of, I reminded myself, taking in several deep breaths until they matched my age and then continued to seek the faces I knew.

There was Sister Agnes, busy with other parents. Yet her kind eyes found mine and smiled into them, putting me at ease. My eyes wandered all over, searching for my classmates. We had gathered by the small refectory where fifth grade and below ate. The rest ate at the next-door bigger, brighter, posher refectory for Big Girls. It even had music playing! Crooked lines had begun to form like puddles shaping into small, seasonal rivers. It suddenly dawned on me that my first-bencher instinct had made me stand at the mouth of the river-line.

I took in the sea of faces behind me, fascinated. What a sight! Little women representing the diversity that is our country, all standing there in one big square. A mini India! In the 1990s, this was a rare sight. Some of their faces revealed the archetypes they had succumbed to: Spoilt Pretty Princesses (very different from Unspoilt Railway Princesses); Loud Ones; Rough and Tough Sporty Types; Caring, Grandmotherly Ones with faces full of love; Aunty Types whose faces revealed their futures even at that young age. What I could not find in that sea was the face of someone who remained alone in a crowd. I realized I had been instinctively seeking out someone just like me. A Coconut Water Craving Railway Princess Misfit.

I didn't find my doppelgänger, but I spotted my first familiar face. A Pretty Princess classmate with silky poker-straight hair that reached till her hips, the longest and prettiest I had ever seen. It was neatly contained in two braids tied with stylishly thin red satin ribbons. All of us wore red ribbons as part of the school uniform. But while hers were pretty, ours were broad, hideous and cheap-looking, fashioned out of awful synthetic material. Curious about which aspect of India her hair represented, I approached her for the first time, for a proper conversation.

'Are you Sikh?' I asked. This could be the only explanation for the length of her hair. The only other girl whose hair was the second-longest after hers had been a girl called Jaspreet, at the school in Vapi. She had told me that she was a Sikh, a *sardarni*, *Surd* for short, but her brother was a custard. That's the part I had not understood. A decade later, while in college, I'd finally be able to figure this out. Her brother was a cut-surd and not a custard.

'Not any more,' she answered.

How weird! She looked a little like Jaspreet. Is this what happens when girls grow their hair too long, too quick? Like Alice who had grown too tall and too short, too quick?

'How come?' I asked.

'I was *sick*!' she replied, looking at me strangely.

I looked at her, even more gobsmacked now. How could one change religions they were born into? In that case, couldn't other aspects of one's identity be changed as well?

It's no use going back to yesterday, because I was a different person then.

She turned her back to me, daintily, not rudely, to continue speaking to her family. Funnily enough, she was speaking in Gujarati! So she was Sikh but now she was Gujarati? How strange! But it wasn't just her. It seemed that most of the girls were Gujarati. The language rained in from every direction possible. Despite living in two Gujarati towns, I had never heard so many people speaking Gujarati all at once.

Perhaps it was because I had lived primarily with the railway crowd. And as everyone knew, in railway colonies — just like those of the armed forces — everybody was from everywhere else. But what little I had experienced of this sweet-natured and gentle-mannered community so far, had made me very fond of them.

Unlike my family, they weren't obsessed with collecting maladies. Or bus tickets.

A girl stood next to me, leaning against the granite parapet of the small refectory. 'Are you Gujarati too?' I asked with a smile. She replied to my friendly question first with a scowl followed immediately afterwards with a poor but powerful axe kick that landed straight on my face. I was shocked, but my body was not. The Tentacle had taught it to be always prepared, ready with the necessary, protective reflexes. My back leg held my weight, a loyal bodyguard preventing me from what could have easily been a concussion.

'Gujarati, my foot!' Finally, she had decided to reply in words. She stared into my eyes like a tough gangster, ensuring that her words remained forever etched in my memory. (They sure did.) 'I am a Rajput! We are Rathores. You remember that.' Her finger in my face withdrew and with that, she returned to leaning against the parapet as if nothing had happened.

This new education baffled me. So far:

1) My only introduction to the Rajput community was the affectionate love I had received from the tough-looking softie brothers, Rana Pratap Singh Kaka and Kana Pratap Singh Kaka.
2) A lot had happened to me within seconds. InPlainSight. Yet it remained an invisible secret.

So many years had passed since the year I had spent with the devils, but their bullying still affected me. Decades later, I'd realize this truth about abuse. Though sexual, physical and domestic abuse got trophies for being the most painful and long-lasting in their effect, the kind of abuse it was didn't really matter. Even the so-called lesser forms of abuse — slaps, kicks, a mean boss, everyday gaslighting and emotional abuse — were just as painful. The devils' form of abuse had made me a bit numb, a bit immune, a bit less naive. It had left me a torn person of many bits whom fresh bullying couldn't damage as much as it should have.

Again, I looked at the sea of people around me. Enlightened by my latest assault, I could suddenly tell the Rajputs apart. Many *sa* sounds broke through the omnipresence of Gujarati, soon revealing themselves to be Rajput suffixes of respect. Books had taught me that in Japan, *san* was a formal suffix of respect, used after a person's name. *Sa* was more out of affection, than as a formal address. *Baisa*, *Dadosa*, *Bhabisa*, *Babosa*, *Dadisa*. My pixie ears also picked up new words like *hukum*, *khama gani*. Nobody asked them, but the kids did a lot of *pranaam*s to their elders — little gestures of respect so effortless, so graceful and most of all, so genuine. Despite the fresh assault, I was completely charmed by Rajput culture.

Almost all the Rajputs at school turned out to be blue-blooded. I wanted to ask so many questions. But the kick warned me that confirming details was unnecessary. Ma'am Ragini of class IV A epitomized this royalty. The kingdoms had long gone, but aristocracy seeped out of them, colouring the evening with a much-needed aura of elegance, an elegance the glowing orange sunset reflected.

When I looked at Madam Rowdy Rathore again, a flash of clairvoyance told me that she'd be a very successful sports captain in the near future. I obviously didn't tell her that. Gentle creatures didn't want to have anything to do with rowdy creatures. From then on, I took every possible step to stay away from Madam Rowdy Rathore.

1) Important Lesson No. 11: One bad apple, in this case Madam Rowdy Rathore, did not define the whole batch.
2) Important Lesson No. 12: Like the devils and Etsektera abusers, you never knew what bully or abuser would crop up where. One always had to be alert.

Fuelled by my brand-new education, I invented a new game: Look at a face and guess their ancestry: a) Gujarati b) Rajput or c) Other.

Important Lesson No.13: Anything could be made into a game. Years later, waiting at the DMV and in hospitals in California, I'd play a 2.0 version of this game guessing what countries people were from.

In that sea of people rose waves of hugs and kisses. A Lack-of-Love tsunami had struck me, taking with it whatever little confidence I had left. Hot salt water burst out of my fiery eyes like lava. Loser tears that only losers know. Another flash of clairvoyance informed me (like MultipleSources would in the future) that it was always going to be like this. That I'd break down out of the blue at the most inconvenient of all spots. That I'd cry at the wrong place at the wrong time for the wrong reasons; defying logic and driving MultipleSources nuts.

Voice of Reason appeared to give a speech: 'You aren't used to this anymore. You were never popular, but at Dimples, you were in a league of your own. The girl with the best grades, the topper with the coolest toys and coolest birthday party, the special girl. You're no longer used to being made to feel invisible. You like to be invisible only when you want to be. You choose your own space now. That's the difference.'

'SHUT UP!' screamed the audience of other voices in chorus, making Voice of Reason's pretty reasonable speech an instant flop show.

Just as she had appeared on my first day at school, Ma'am Amita appeared out of nowhere on my first day at boarding school too. As on that day and the others that had followed, she brought with her, her usual cheer and warmth, putting me at ease. I smiled at her through my evaporated tears. Perhaps sensing my gloom, she sprinkled some 'power' on me. For children, this meant being entrusted with responsibilities that involved authority.

'Make a list of all the girls in the class for me,' she instructed. I looked at the huge wild rock behind her. Beyond it was the cemented playground at the edge of which were the teachers' cottages, where she lived.

'Of fifth standard girls, Ma'am?' I asked smiling, faking confidence.

'No. Second standard!' she said.

('See how someone with "Actual Power" trusts you? This should give you the confidence to discover your Own Power. Once you have discovered that, your own power will trickle on to other things.' Voice of Reason interrupted with another speech, silencing other voices in the audience. Decades would pass before Voice of Reason or I and perhaps many in the audience themselves would realize that Own Power was simply owning the void within. For now, Voice of Reason's reasonable speech became an instant hit show.)

The frown on my face gave away the fact that I had become serious. I was so new here. Where and how would I find second grade? And why now? I was already so exhausted from the events of the evening.

'But, Ma'am, I don't know where to find them.'

'Du-uh. Sweetheart, fifth standard, obviously! Grow a sense of humour.' She patted my hair, smiling kindly, her eyes full of mischief.

This was my first at processing sarcasm. I had pretty much taken everything and everyone at face value before, as children do. We believe everything to be the truth, that is until we are taught what is a joke according to grown-ups, older siblings and other influencers. Perhaps this is what they call innocence. Each child outgrows it at her own pace, depending on the level of conditioning she has had. Being left alone, I had had little conditioning and so, in the fifth grade, I was at the level of a six-year-old. I realized for the very first time that grown-ups lie even out of goodness or kindness. And that sarcasm is considered humour! I didn't really like it, but I processed it like anybody in the business of growing up has to.

What was important now was that Ma'am Amita had appeared as the familiar warm face I was seeking. My loneliness evaporated.

A shrill bell rang announcing that it was time for dinner.

'Do it later!' she said. 'And Ritu, welcome!' She smiled before disappearing.

The bell was the first symbol which differentiated the Small Girls from the Big Girls. Ours was the size of a *pooja* bell, reflecting the size of our power. It was light enough to be lifted by just three fingers. The Big Girls' bell was loud, huge and heavy, needing to be carried with both hands. Both bells served the same purpose, summoning us into lines, ending whatever resemblance we had to rivers swollen in the rain, flooding freely everywhere. It struck me then that living in Boarding meant living in even more lines than at Dimples.

Dinner turned out to be a strange yellow puddle that had already been ladled onto plates. The tables on which the plates rested themselves were unique — grey-white tabletops held upon green wooden legs. There were three long rows of these, with matching long green benches. The tables were laid out properly with forks and spoons. There were even little baskets holding many tiny cloth squares, each rolled up inside a colourful plastic baby bangle. Outside of a restaurant, I had never seen tables laid out so properly. A mild but awful damp smell wafted in from God Knows Where, ruining whatever appetite I could have mustered for these mysterious liquids. Even our drinking water had a strange pinkish hue. I discovered later that this was so because it was medicated for our protection.

The bell rang again and everyone burst out together into a sweet poem.

Bless us, o Lord,
and these thy gifts which we are about to receive from thy bounty
through Christ our Lord.
Amen.

Only everyone's hands were joined. Why? Was this a prayer? I asked my neighbour what this was. 'Grace!' she said. What a pretty word I thought. Then I remembered that some children at Dimples Hostel, too, did something similar. They were saying grace! But their poem sounded easier and it actually rhymed!

Thank you for the world so sweet.
Thank you for the food we eat.
God bless our food.
Amen.

The girls grabbed those pieces of cloth and, removing the bangles, wore the cloth like necklaces. The napkins were worn as bibs by the Small Girls and placed on laps by the Big Girls.

The mysterious liquid turned out to be plain old simple daal. Not as delicious as Comfort Food Menu, but somewhat okay. It was also my first time scooping it up from a flat plate. I guess that's what education is — an endless series of firsts. It was followed by yet another first for me, a dish I had not heard of until now (and never would, post Boarding) — macaroni *subzi*. It was yucky!

Another mysterious yellow liquid that had to be scooped up with spoons from plates now greeted us. What was this stinginess? Had they run out of bowls?

Or were they all taken for use by the higher powers who also had MovieChoosingPowers in the hall next door? But I stopped thinking the moment I tasted the second liquid. It was yummy! At last, a delicious first! I asked my neighbours what it was. It turned out to be something they called porridge. I was content with the answer then. I wouldn't discover, until many years later, that this was actually my first taste of something I had read about many times — good, old-fashioned yellow custard. Wow, it wasn't a person after all.

The *pooja* bell melodiously announced the end of dinner. It was time to return to our lines. We met Sister Sarah. Like the school itself, the building was bifurcated — this time by a flight of stairs. On the left were the two dormitories where us 'smallies' lived. On the right were the numerous dormitories where Big Girls, those in sixth standard and up, lived happily ever after, enjoying their power and freedom. On the left were Aurora and Dawn. On the right were Eos, Tulip and other poetic places.

Sister Sarah was in charge of us. I was in Dawn, the bigger of the smallies' dorms. At this point, however, the residents of both Aurora and Dawn were equals. We arranged our supplies, then handed them over to Sister Sarah for safekeeping in her huge wooden cupboard by the wall. She locked it with one out of a huge bunch of keys she carried everywhere. Sister Sarah was neither pleasant nor unpleasant — just plain businesslike. We gave her all our toiletries for safekeeping, keeping only what was absolutely needed — one tube of toothpaste, one soap, one shampoo, one talcum powder tower, one tin of

Nivea, Etsektera. A group of ones. Whenever anything ran out, we'd go to her and she'd open the almirah with one key from her bunch, look for our boarding school numbers, and hand out the item we needed from our set.

The Margo soap with 291 lay in my hands like a baby bird. I put it on top of my locker, trying to erase the stinging sudsy memories it held in spite of its innocence. 'It's only soap. Don't overthink,' cautioned Voice of Reason. I put it away, focusing on the blue Nivea tin instead, opening it, then peeling off its aluminium foil curtain and inhaling its wonderfully comforting, clean fragrance, allowing it to wash all over me, cleansing what the soap never could.

In the fifth standard, we began to use ink pens. I had only ugly Camlin ones. Neither my father nor me were aware that in the uniformed world of boarding schools, everything that wasn't in uniform was automatically a fashion statement, a metric of one's coolness and status, of one's worth. And so I found that everyone else had cool China pens or pens from countries I had only seen in the Atlas. Countries like Taiwan, Zambia, Kenya, Saudi Arabia, UAE, Etsektera. By Grace of God, some equality did prevail because everybody had to use Camel fountain ink. A huge relief.

My basic toiletries were an embarrassment compared to brands like Sunsilk, Fa, Suave, Jergens, Etsektera, that everyone else seemed to have. I was so thankful that apart from our nightwear, we changed from uniform to uniform continuously. Can you imagine the shame I'd have had to face if 'coloured clothes', the name for regular clothes, were not just meant for Sundays and a few special days but for all days?

Sister Antoine, who was also Sister Superior (a post, like a school principal's but for the boarding school) taught us grammar. One afternoon, hers was the last period. The bell rang. As everyone rushed out into freedom with the speed of raindrops, she called me out. She collected her things and asked me to walk with her back towards the buildings that were our living quarters.

'You know, Reetoo, you're the reason I enjoy teaching this class so much,' she said casually. 'So thank you, child!'

I might as well have been struck by lightning. Praise, a completely normal vitamin most children's grown-ups had supplemented them heavily with, was like desert rain for me. And here it was, coming to me casually from the boss of all the authority figures in my world! How was I supposed to react? What had I done in that land of tenses, modal verbs and clauses, that had made me stand out?

'Why, Sister?' I mumbled guiltily. She looked at me, slightly startled. The shock I had felt must have oozed out of my words and pores.

'Well, you are the one who keeps asking all those questions. You make me think of unique examples and exceptions, making it interactive...like a game! It was great fun!' she said. I smiled. She put her arm lovingly on my skinny shoulders and walked me towards the boarding area.

And so, I remained the teacher's pet. Outside class, I was rather quiet. There was nobody to talk to. Luckily, I got so lost in routine, lines, hymns and prayer rituals that it didn't really matter.

The girls came alive at teatime. Myriad treats jumped out like genies from aluminium and steel treasure tuck boxes, bringing with them, memories of home, and parts of themselves they had locked away, unawares. Biscuits, candy, deep-fried homemade snacks of spiced up or sweetened wheat and chickpea flours, deep-fried lentil snacks, pickles... I learned new synonyms for joy — *bhujia*, *namkeen*, *churan*. *Khakra* was the only thing familiar in my tuck box. The wafer-thin savoury snacks had cracked during their long ride from home. I wasn't so fond of them, but they were a taste of home and of the kind old lady who sold them at the railway station as a side business along with her full-time railway job of manning the drinking water area. She always wore a blue saree uniform, fed me *khakra* and asked me what I was up to. *Khakra* at school brought back warm memories of a time when I was a little less lonely. The other contents of my tuck box were factory-made goodies foreign to me that Pup-Pa had bought quickly — since I had no preference — at the local grocery store. These had been chosen randomly; they carried no memories. I did not know then that these Bikaji snacks were a clean slate I was now writing new memories on, the start of a lifelong love for *bhujia* and all things *chatpata*.

Smriti Singh was our 'minder' at night time. This was when, at the end of a long day, dressed in our comfortable pyjamas and nighties, we studied in bed. I loved studying in my cozy Reading Room, the walls of which were made of my pillow on the back with adjacent bedside lockers on both sides. My feet were stretched out on the blanket floor, in my imaginary garden. With this compact world, I was subconsciously simulating the same need for comfort that toddlers and pets have when they enter cardboard boxes.

Being human and only a child, Smriti Singh would often misuse her superpower through surprise punishments. People who upset her had to kneel on the cold hard floor facing all of us on our comfortable beds. Of course, we stared at them like they were zoo animals. By night-time, most of us were simply too tired to feel humiliation at any surprise punishment. The unfortunate girls who were chosen for this happened to be either those who were found to be talking when they were not supposed to, even if it was only for a second about something necessary like 'Can you move your feet, so I can walk out?' Or as in my case, found to be asleep, when I should have been awake. I became a regular, each time astounded to be told that I had fallen asleep. They were lying. I knew I had been awake! My focus went from studying to being alert and awake. Naturally, my academic performance began to suffer.

This twisted hierarchy of putting children in charge of other children created a ground ripe for emotional abuse. It was cruel and completely unnecessary. I got my first taste of political power dynamics that Pup-Pa often complained about and probably faced daily. It was a great lesson to cope with the Real World Outside.

On birthdays, democracy prevailed like pots of Camlin ink. We boarders always got two types of Parle sugar-boiled sweets to distribute. One was a delicious orange flavour, the other, an even more delicious yellow candy called Zing Zang, with a zesty lemon flavour. Everyone gobbled these immediately, but I'd always save mine, choosing to relish them slowly, privately, when I desperately needed sweetness to survive the countless discomforts in my apparently comfortable life. Such as on a bad night when Smriti Singh had punished me.

Or when everybody else had received letters from home, save me. Letters and trunk calls were indeed getting less and less frequent as Pup-Pa got more and more immersed in his world of union politics. Apparently, everyone else knew this Important Fact about me; I was a kind of minor celebrity — the girl who always has sweets, even as we have none.

I was blissfully unaware of my fame till one evening when I was desperately pinching myself to stay awake to avoid any punishments for falling asleep. I was poking myself with the top part of a used ball pen. This was a trick I had just learned in which you can extend the usable life of a small, dying pencil by tucking it inside the top half of a pen — it looked like a cigarette holder extending the life of a heroine's cigarette in the movies. This was recycling, Indian style, back in the '90s.

It had been a tough evening. During dinner, several neighbours had been called. Their legs turned into wings, as they partly ran and partly flew as fast as they could to the nuns' quarters to take their urgent trunk calls. Honestly, that's what we all lived for — these calls, letters and tuck boxes, all reminders that we were beloved princesses, Spoilt Pretty Princesses, and not lesser mortals with barely any choices. They would return beaming, wearing invisible crowns like halos around their head. My name, of course, was not called. Yet again.

I was really fed up.

1) Fed up of rules.
2) Fed up of changing from one uniform to another.
3) Fed up of standing in endless lines.

I missed the less glamorous hostel I had just left to be here in this dream place. I needed a Zing Zang.

I unlocked my locker and pulled out my stash of sweets. As I moved back, I bumped into something soft. Standing just behind me was Smriti Singh with a pleading look in her eyes. 'Please, just one!' she begged, looking at the Zing Zangs in my hand as if her life depended on them. The authority figure was begging from the beggar! Unable to help myself, I broke out into laughter. 'Please, please. Just one,' she pleaded. 'Please. Please!' I was tempted to give in. 'N O!' said the voice, reminding me that I had unexpectedly stumbled upon a very rare moment of 'Own Power'. 'No,' I repeated confidently. 'Sorry!' I added.

An hour after Smriti Singh had left, the high of the power trip extinguished, turning into shame. This could not be Own Power. A part of me had often wished to have my string of abusers end up as beggars. Grateful that the enormous space in my life had enabled such awareness so as to make me feel guilty about my behaviour, I left two Zing Zangs on Smriti Singh's bed the next morning. The treasures were safely hidden in the tiny valley between her pillow and an elevation on the checkered counterpane that each bed had. Only someone close enough or on the bed, itself, could have spotted the sweets. I don't know if she got them or not. We never spoke about it. But she never punished me ever again.

In the lines where we did so much of our living, I found an unexpected friend in my classmate, Arohi. Just like that, we made up another Charlie Chaplin dance that we began to perform first in the line, and later began to greet each other with when we met. We stretched our legs, holding what I'd discover decades later was a horse pose in yoga. We'd shake one leg wildly, while still holding the pose with the other, then alternate the legs to walk in huge exaggerated steps, bursting into laughter as we danced. Only we found this amusing. These spontaneous moments of childlike innocence were pretty much what our friendship consisted of. At that time, it was more than enough. I don't know about her but it brought me much happiness and reminded me that I was still a child.

At the corner of every dormitory was a generous square space that was curtained off. It was a room of sorts which we longed to peek into and which we were convinced was palatial and better than Narnia. Inside it, lived the matron assigned to the dorm. In Dawn, it was Sister Sarah. In Aurora, it was a spinster we called Ma'am. Our matron was Ma'am Milissa, whose kindness was reserved strictly for her flatterers. She was obsessed with blessing people, often painting invisible crosses on their eager foreheads with holy water. She'd close her eyes and mumble, 'I bless you (the girl's name).' The entire dormitory would queue up willingly, clearly more eager for the benefits of being in Ma'am Milissa's good books, than in her blessings.

I'd watch, completely mesmerized by the drama — till the day I discovered that Ma'am Milissa had two categories of blessings. There were the regular ones and there was the special one with double the intensity of thc blessings, reserved for special people. In an almost trance-like, borderline-possessed state, with quivering, half-closed eyes, she would call upon the Father, the Son, and the Holy Spirit, ensuring she had woken them up with her scary drama. Then, she'd pierce the centre of the child's forehead as if digging a tunnel there for the Holy Trinity to enter them right away. It was a miracle that no one ever fell down from the sheer metaphysical power of the Holy Trinity or from the physical power being drilled into them.

This was my first proper exposure to religion. One of the consequences of practically raising myself was that I had been left unadulterated from much conditioning, including the ways of the world and religion. Brand new concepts, all important enough to begin with capital letters, wafted into my daily awareness. Concepts like Heaven and Hell, God, Father, Son and the Holy Spirit. Apart from Grace, we said endless prayers like 'Our Father', 'Hail Mary' and my favourite, 'Remember O' most gracious Virgin Mary'. There was something comforting about them. So comforting that I began to say 'Remember O' most gracious Virgin Mary' to myself as I hid with my books by the pigsty at the far corner of the campus, far away from where *Kho Kho* was being played. (And Rowdy Rathore, true to my prediction, was one of the Small Girls' leaders.)

Somewhere in these moments of comfort, in the thrill of appreciation from my teachers, in the extreme sorrow of rejection and isolation, and living day after day in the lines, the year went by. Vacation time dawned on us, filling Aurora with such joy! It was as if the very Aurora Borealis had bathed Aurora with its magnificence.

Our holidays were bunched up together strategically, so that we were spared the three most unforgiving months of the year, when winter was at its most bitter in the mountains. Everybody packed up in delight. The whole campus burst with celebration and freedom as child after child left with beaming parents. As always, I watched.

Important Lesson No.14: There were Livers and there were Watchers. The Tentacle had turned me into a Watcher, watching over my body and others as if life were a movie. Always hiding, always far off, always watching.

Except for a handful of us, everybody left. Maids, whom we called didis also remained, some reluctantly so, because if we — their work — remained, their time off was curtailed. Most of the didis were kind, but a few loved to gossip at our expense, some not even giving us the dignity of doing so behind our backs. One was especially vile. I hated calling her 'didi', big sister.

'Your father has dumped you here. He is now a free bird,' she told me to my face. It was my first time of being subjected to a completely new kind of emotional abuse. Her venom consumed me; it stung even more because it was probably true. Was this all it took for lies to turn into truths? You simply spoke things into existence, and voilà, they became facts? M had done it, said the scar on my right eyebrow. 'What choice did M have?' asked Voice of Reason. An urgent need to protect the most important adult in my life came over me. (All children do this. Another example of the several invisible responsibilities that children bear.)

'No. My father loves me. He is busy working for the rights of railway workers,' I said, choking, swallowing the tears that threatened to well up. 'Workers like yourself, Meana Didi, but who are far more needy.'

'*Haan, haan*. We can see that,' she sniggered as she folded the tall pile of counterpanes in front of her. 'He is serving people and thinking you are happy here. No responsibility. No obstacles.'

I walked away, the burning tears flowing freely now. There were too many things to process:

1) It's one thing that adults don't get you. It's another thing that adults taunt you.
2) How could I tell her that happiness was a very small thing compared to safety, which was everything. No matter what, I was safe here in a way I never was at home.
3) I had only known the labour class as being extremely kind. This was the first time I was seeing this side of them.

   Important Lesson No. 15: Truly nothing and nobody could be defined or generalized.
4) Not only could the labour class be unnecessarily nasty, they could also be the actual ones in power. This was weirdly true in our world. Our fees paid their salaries. Yet we had to suck up to them in small ways (such as flattery and agreement), which gave them a sense of authority, even a sense of power over us. This was an interesting role reversal.

I couldn't wait to get away from Meana Didi, the smelly small refectory and Ma'am Milissa's blessing fetish. That night, as she drilled blessings into my third eye, 'In the name of the Father, the Son and the Holy Spirit,' I wished for a brighter, saner, happier sixth grade.

The next afternoon, the half-a-dozen of us smallies gathered in Dawn where Sister Sarah gave us a rare treat — movies. Throughout those days and through others, us leftovers watched the only three movies available to us — the jarring Bollywood film *Beta*, the lovely *The Sound of Music* and the religious *Jesus of Nazareth*. In *Beta*, the kid playing Anil Kapoor's role when he is a child, calls his mother in heaven when she dies. A telephone operator with ample Vitamin Kindness, or Vitamin K, which Meana Didi was so deficient in — and Ma'am Amita, Ma'am Ragini and Aunty Kipling so abundant in — pretends to be his mother and tells him that she'll come to visit him soon. The line of little heads watching *Beta* automatically turned to gaze at me, showering me with pitying glances — *Maahaara love*. Girls would give me the same look when hymns like *Mother of Mine* were played or sung.

Important Lesson No. 16: People think Pity is Love. But the pitied know that Pity is not Love.

I complained to Sister Marie, an adorable Irish-American nun bursting with Vitamin Kindness, who taught kindergarten. She was my favourite person at Boarding. I had begun to escape games time by going to her and helping her prepare question papers for the kindergarteners. This would mean a calm couple of hours cutting and pasting pictures of tiny apples and oranges to form cute equations like 2+2 in pictures.

Important Lesson No. 17: Sitting relaxed next to someone in silence (mostly) and doing your thing is the Feeling of Love.

Smiling, she suggested I pray to Mother Mary, the protector of children. The next evening, she placed something cold and hard in my palm and closed my hand over it. 'Here, my child.' In my palm was an ivory statue of a woman I knew. 'This is Mother Mary. She is everybody's mother. She is your mother from now on.' Total acceptance, also known as the Feeling of Love swept over me. I began to cry. What kind of tears were these? Was it Mama Mary's love? Or was it Sister Marie's love? 'Does it matter?' answered the Voice of Reason.

More parents must have come to take their kids home because when I returned, even fewer of us leftovers remained. They were watching my favourite, *The Sound of Music* — the one sane choice between our other two extreme options — one a religious movie, and the other that made the adult-rated '*Dhak dhak...*' ring in our ears for days.

I thought of Dimples, where physical space was scarce. Here at Boarding, the campus was huge. But there were far too many processes and rules and prayers. The syllabus wasn't getting any easier, either, and it was getting harder and harder for me to study in the little time allocated every day. My grades dipped, but somehow, I held on to my fifth rank. This was still the highest a Boarder — without the supplemental support of parental Love, tuition, extra hours of study and Etsektera privileges — had scored that year. Naturally, I continued to remain a favourite of the nuns and the teachers. Result Time divided us into two groups:

Group 1: Those who got a first division, distinction and best-of-all, a rank.

Group 2: Those who had failed in a subject.

Mysterious forces settled everyone into a long line which went in all directions, enough to confuse a snake colony. Each girl held out her hand to the god/nun in charge of placing their fates on their respective small palms, as if doling out *prasad*. A bar of chocolate fell into each Group 1 palm. A humble WMD, a wooden ruler, fell into each Group 2 palm. Giggles, cries, ouches, giggles. Giggles, cries, ouches, giggles. Boarding was shrouded in an impromptu concert with a catchy beat.

Just when I had given up on him ever arriving, Pup-Pa arrived. I was the third-last girl to be picked up during that break. As I walked down the slope with him, I realized how much I had changed. I had been so lost in Meana Didi's projections and the collective wish for everybody to go home that I had forgotten my own preference. The truth was that I didn't even want to go home! I knew just what I could expect at home. At best, it would be another holiday by myself, without the hustle and bustle of being around hundreds of children.

Pup-Pa, too, had changed. He had become quiet, withdrawn, distracted and increasingly inaccessible to me. When he did communicate, he seemed hyper, aggressive and snapped easily saying something like, 'What do you know?' or 'You're just a child.' His rare letters had made me aware of the pressure of union politics. But something more had obviously happened. I made one last heroic attempt to get it out of him. 'Pup-Pa, what's wrong?'

'Try running three households. Plus, union pressures. Then you'll know.'

Although I knew nothing about running households, I knew the world of railway trade unions well, so much so that I suspect my first words might have been Pay Commission, Comrade and Morcha. Saying nothing more, both of us looked out of the jeep taxi as it went downhill on the rickety slopes. I felt bad for him. Part of me was relieved this version of him was not visiting me.

Quiet afternoons slumbered on in Vapi. Two *kakas*, one unusually short, and the other unusually tall, both named Periaswamy, ran after me as I learned to bicycle without training wheels, like the Railway Princess I was. (Afterwards, I would have coconut water.)

One afternoon, the postman brought an envelope with my marksheet. Holding my breath like those who know it isn't good news, I tore the envelope open. Indeed, I had gotten just 72 per cent, missing distinction by just three percentiles. Pup-Pa would be furious. 'But only if he found out,' said Voice of Reason. I tore up the result like I had torn its cover a few moments ago. Later that evening, when the sweeper lady arrived to burn a small pile of rubbish, mostly dried leaves, I threw in the pieces, ensuring that the result turned into ash.

On another late afternoon, when I returned home from my delightful bicycle ride around the colony, loud chatter echoed out of the living room. I parked my bicycle in the front yard as usual and walked close to the custard yellow front door, peering in. Happiness instantly evaporated. Fright poured in to replace it. There he was — S Sir chatting with Pup-Pa. The Tentacle squeezed my defective heart. WholeHeartWithaHole banged with escalating fury, demanding to be let out. Immediately! I hid by the apricot tree in the side-yard, safely out of sight, in a joyful place where I had recently made a magical discovery. An apricot seed held an almond inside like a pearl inside an oyster! So what if this almond was bitter? It was still cool! Now, as this place of magic sheltered me, it transformed into a spot of terror. Like the guava tree.

Important Lesson No. 17: Prison was better than vacations.

Should I tell Pup-Pa? He had ousted Uncle At at only a suspicion. S Sir was a real abuser. He'd probably throw him out. Imagining S Sir thrashed made me smile in delight.

'N O! N O W A Y!' screamed Voice of Reason. Right as always, was Voice of Reason. Pup-Pa seemed happy here with his friends and more of his old self. I suppose that's what friends do to you. I ran and ran and ran, falling, scraping my knees, sullying my frock, getting up and running once again. I stopped and looked around. I was no longer in Railway Colony! I was on the main road, where I wasn't ever supposed to venture out alone. In front of me was Vapi General Store. Not quite knowing why, I entered the shop. The shopkeeper knew me and smiled. His smile looked creepy. Warning bells louder than fire alarms rang in my head. This must be how S Sir spotted his victims. I ran back, past the house of my 'best friend'. (A girl called Heena, the only other kid my age in the colony, whom I had decided to feature in stories I invented. Stories I could tell Meana Didi to show that I had a rich, well-rounded, loving life full of besties and a father who taught his daughter to ride a bike.) I ran and ran till finally, I reached Rai Aunty's house. She saw me and invited me in, warmly. '*Esho Mona. Esho.*' Ignoring the obvious, my unusually dishevelled appearance, she gestured me to sit at her dining table. I couldn't be more grateful for her Vitamin Kindness.

'Taste this!' she said, patting my hair and giving me a spoon and a small steel bowl with a mysterious dark something in it. 'This batch just got ready,' she said. I obliged. It was the sweetest lime pickle I had ever had! And the most delicious. With just a mild tang to it, it might as well have been Zing Zang. The Taste of Escape.

The sweetness I craved came in myriad forms. Zing Zangs, mother figures and friendships appeared of their own accord. The candy-like *aachaar* made me realize how perfect everything was in its own way. School was safer than home. Wasn't it ideal then that Pup-Pa didn't pick me up during the smaller holidays? That he came late during the big winter break?

Was this the grace I needed? Was this what the nuns called Salvation?

11

Sixth Grade

Fortunately, all things end and this one big holiday did too. At the school gates, I screamed a silent Hallelujah, grateful for what had earlier annoyed me. Strict routines, lines, rules, uniforms, prayers and dorms were now my comfort zones. Sixth grade was a new beginning in many ways. I was now officially a Big Girl. I was no longer on the radar of mean didis, messed-up minders or crazy matrons. This promotion was automatic. Like all of nature's gifts, I had done nothing to earn it or deserve it.

Our drinking water though, continued to remain coloured, either pinkish or yellowish, unmindful of the status of its drinkers. The medication kept us safe from water-borne illnesses and Etsektera germs. But its stench and flavour meant that many of us, including me, could barely drink any, causing severe constipation. A few unreported cases lasted for a record 11 days! Quack remedies came to the rescue. *Hajmola*, *churan*, even a magical potion called *divel* (which turned out to be good old castor oil from somebody's farm).

Medication trickled into strange places. A mild chemical, rumoured to be DDT, was mixed into coconut oil to prevent an invasion of lice. Didis, mean and nice, drenched every inch of our scalps and hair with this magical remedy. It worked like a charm, keeping us from being clones of the *langurs* on campus, who loved to spend their afternoons sitting in rows, lustily picking lice from the head of the *langur* (often, a younger one) seated in front. Of course, they were gross enough to immediately pop the lice and lice eggs into their mouths, as if their mouths were the closest dustbins. It was also one of the few times the *langurs* sat peacefully. Otherwise, anything from a toothy smile to the sight of a rare packet of chips in our hands was enough for them to grab and then, fight among themselves, like only monkeys can. Unlike my favourite monkeys — orangutans (technically, apes) — who had soulful eyes and matching ways, our neighbours here in the hills were uncouth, unkind and petty.

Many of us had learned to self-medicate with whatever drug we could find to soothe ourselves all InPlainSight, like toddlers who insist on putting dangerous things into their mouths. The bravest of us chewed on staple pins. The relatively normal ate chalk — the most popular option. I'm not sure whether this was because of its abundance, easy access and portability, or because of its social acceptability or comparative familiarity in taste and texture (to real medicines). The poshest option, which I favoured, was chewing on ink-free plain paper. (Years later in California, squirrels relishing trash pizza in a sea of natural, organic acorns would teach me that despite what grown-ups said, it was perfectly normal for NotFood to be Food and Food to be NotFood.)

Some nuns abundant in Vitamin K figured out our addictions and asked us to identify why we did it. They thought calcium would take care of chalk. Physical exercises like running would take care of the need to chew on metal. Fiber intake would take care of paper cravings. They, like the addicts themselves, had no idea that the deficiencies were not merely physical, and that like compulsive shoppers and consumers, we too were trying to soothe ourselves, trying to fill voids within us that we didn't know existed.

On the heels of medication, came new vocabulary — terms so innocent that they couldn't be used in the Real World Outside:

1. *Occupy:* From reserving a bathroom, to a spot on a bench, to a place in the line, to bagging a portion of a favourite food, anything could be occupied. Temporary ownership was declared in terms that defied the laws of tense and grammar: 'I occupy; you occupy; she occupy.'
2. *Hurry Upping:* I was always corrected when I said, 'I was hurrying up.'
3. *Tattle:* Almost always used as a word for gossip: I/she/you tattled or will tattle. It was also used as a threat to show power if conditions were not obeyed: I will tattle your name to _______.
4. *Cock (as a suffix):* Tattlecock, fightercock, shuttlecock, studycock, and countless other derivatives.
5. *Slow Coach:* Showing you were faster and, therefore, superior by using this homegrown term as a legal swear word.
6. *Piglet:* A major swear word.
7. *Bloody:* Bloody was a prefix to and for anything: Bloody Bombayite / Gujju / Rajput. Or worse, just you itself: You Bloody...

8. *Forfeit:* You lost out on the few privileges you had, like Sunday treats, because a higher power had reported you for being naughty.
9. *Naughty:* A synonym for talking at the wrong place at the wrong time. Grown-ups did it all the time. 'How is talking naughty?' I'd ask Pup-Pa and he'd say, 'Because it is naughty!' and proceed to give another speech.

Located neither in the smallies' dorms — Aurora and Dawn — nor in the mysterious dorms of the Big Girls located opposite them, my new dorm, Periwinkle, was a sort of bardo in itself. Like me, Periwinkle was an outcast, a misfit located at the shadowy back end of everyone's living quarters, almost as if in the underworld. If it ever flooded, Periwinkle would be the first to go. Yet, the light-starved residence was closer to the divine than all the others. Above it was the serene, spacious, light-filled chapel, a desperately needed source of peace accessible at all hours. On Periwinkle's immediate left, almost at its entrance, lay suspended in mid-air the thickest, strongest and the most timeless iron chain I'd ever seen, almost waiting to be pulled. It wasn't an ordinary train chain and one only had to look up to realize its importance. It was the only access to the timeless and gigantic Angelus bell hanging two storeys above. This mammoth chain was the closest thing to Jack's beanstalk that I'd ever seen in real life. When invisible forces rung the giant bell at dawn, noon, dusk and during special holy hours to summon nuns into prayer, its sound washed all over us, putting us into a silent, tranquil trance that lasted well after it had stopped ringing. I remained sensitive to sounds — perhaps Saralipi's leftovers — but no sound since has ever had the same effect on me.

Periwinkle's matron was older, chubbier and most importantly, much saner than Ma'am Milissa, and without a blessing fetish. She was kind, gentle, private and quiet and insisted on being called Aunty instead of Ma'am. In spite of her big size, she never quite occupied a space fully. Instead, she somehow blended into the space, becoming invisible. Her thinning hair, pale skin and soft voice made her appear more like a timid bird than a matron. So long as we were quiet and well-behaved, she'd retire to her curtained square. Through the gaps, we could see a small statue of my beloved Mama Mary. Often, I would see her counting the beads on her rosary and murmuring the accompanying prayers. The comfort her favourite accessory brought to her was obvious to all because she was almost never seen without it. She never imposed prayers on us. I respected her for having the grace to keep her spirituality private. On my walks to help Sister Marie, I would often find Aunty Amelia at the grotto — so deeply immersed in her spiritual world that she didn't notice that I, who should have been at the playground, was breaking a rule right under her nose. Grace was rare in that world and Aunty Amelia's effortless grace made me naturally respect her.

We no longer studied on our beds and, therefore, there was no need for Smriti Singh's post. We studied in a place fit for Big Girls — in a big study hall behind the Angelus bell. The room was even bigger than the dining hall and some 200 of us studied in pin-drop silence. We had our own desks, chairs and even shelves in shared cupboards for storing our books. We were even granted an extra hour in the mornings for studying. These should have ensured that we did well, but we did not as our studies had gotten more complex and overwhelming. We desperately needed extra tutoring but had zero external guidance. The school's teachers were sincere, but relatively mediocre in their teaching skills. So, really, very few of us were performing spectacularly. My own percentage began to plummet — the first few beads in a string of lifelong failures. But, just as with the cycles of abuse, I did not know that yet.

Abuse was the perfect metric to measure all of life's uncertainties. I continued to work more diligently than ever before, lapping up all the study guides I could forage. But no matter how hard I tried, the concepts in the books made no sense.

One evening, I discovered Sister Marie had left. Sister Agnes revealed that she had been taken to the big hospital where she was battling cancer. 'Our Lady is watching over her. But she needs our prayers, child,' she said. The need for unnecessary strength in her voice told me much more than her words did. When grown-ups feel the need to be strong in front of children, it means that they are either completely broken or defeated, often both. I knew then that there was very little hope of Sister Marie's recovery. Sorrow washed over me. Some girls had dolls, some babies had pacifiers, some dogs had blankets, Aunty Amelia had a rosary. I had the tiny statue. I clutched it with all the lack in the world I knew. Once again, a loved one was leaving my life — like fake pearls in a cheap pearl necklace, falling off one by one.

Sister Marie had introduced me to Mother Mary, but now it was her absence which brought me closer to her. I spent a lot of my free time in the chapel by a statue of the Virgin Mary. Peace flooded me. A type of peace I could barely remember and yet, it was one which I knew. The feeling of being back by my beloved peepul. The Feeling of Love.

We were now too big to play *Kho Kho* and too small to play basketball. The sport that fit our Goldilocks-like situation best was dodgeball. But balls still petrified me, so this sport was sheer terror. From the time I woke up, I would plan my evening escape.

1) I could wander off to the pigsty area. Nobody was bound to find me there.
2) I could hide in the primary school area. Specifically in the balcony of class IV A and IV B. Nobody ever came upstairs.
3) I could go to the chapel.

Both at the pigsty and in the balcony, I studied. But the last option, usually my most desperate, soon became my favourite. It had a wonderful side-effect. Even if a nun caught me here, she'd probably smile in approval and speak gently, trying to disguise her approval instead of punishing me. Dodging dodgeball for most of sixth grade, with the same zeal that the nuns had for religion, was a big chapter in a lifetime of skipping sports.

By now, I'd made a host of General Friends, playing as children normally do, with any child they meet.

Around me though, this trait was fading as we in sixth grade began to walk out of childhood and walk towards puberty. Etsektera grew up into etcetera. Deep, solid friendships were being born, forming almost monogamous bonds with their Best Friends or in the small groups they were loyal to. I was liked by all, but close to none. (Not yet.)

One evening, we were playing Uno cards by the single step beside the Angelus bell chain. I was the only one with a pack of Uno cards and the girls were delighted that I had shared my cards with them. A new face with big sad eyes and short blunt-cut hair so thick that it could be a sweater, appeared. 'Come play with us,' I called out. Without a word, she joined in. Everyone noticed her colourful backpack (so obviously imported) with a real working clock embedded in it. I had never seen a school bag like that before (or after). But it was her quietness that I noticed. By deciding upon a favourite friend (who would turn into a Best Friend for life) I grew up in that moment. Of course, I didn't know that yet.

Another new girl with a huge backpack appeared. Her quiet ways, too, made her stand out from the rest. The novels her black bag held like secrets, though, gave her away. Here was the only other bookworm besides myself. We became friends instantly (not knowing then that she would leave the very next year, in spite of which, we would remain close friends for life), discussing, exchanging and reading copies of illustrated classics. She introduced me to *Little Women*. It sowed in me a new, deep longing for the safety that is sisterhood. Something I became jealous of instantly because I didn't have it.

I introduced her to Jules Verne and H.G. Wells. Some weeks later, it struck Diya and me, that she, Noor and I had become female versions of the musketeers in *The Three Musketeers*. Even though we befriended others, we were inseparable. During the official weekend evening walks around town, we softly parodied corny Hindi movie songs like 'Yeh dosti hum nahee todenge', swearing our eternal friendship with the innocence of 11-year-olds. It was a wonderful feeling to finally fit in and belong.

Without realizing it, we had formed a ritual of walking in the playground at dusk, during the brief breather we had after dinner. Both of them would run all the way. I'd follow at the pace of my defective heart, listening to the murmurs of my WholeHeartWithAHole. Venus shone above us like home, brighter than all the stars. Did Tentacles exist on Venus? 'No, not here,' she whispered.

My nose began to live a life of its own, a way of life it would continue until I had birthed life myself. Like with the cycles of abuse, I did not know that yet. As my sense of smell dimmed, my nose bled out of the blue, at the most inconvenient of all times — like when I was on stage, answering in class, running late, etcetera. It would bleed with vigour, refusing to stop until half a dozen handkerchiefs were sufficiently drenched beyond repair, until everyone around had been sufficiently scandalized. Fixated on the symptom itself, they had no idea that my nose was leaking secrets, secrets I had kept hidden InPlainSight.

One evening, a letter arrived for me. As usual, my friends ran and waited for me. I walked even more slowly that day. 'What's wrong?' my friend asked. 'You should be thrilled, you finally got a letter,' said my other friend kindly. I looked up with hot tears that had flowed onto the envelope, making an illegible tiny inky puddle. They looked puzzled. 'It's from him,' I explained. It was from P. A jovial letter from an uncle to his beloved niece. A Normal letter filling in Normal details about a Normal uncle and his Normal family, asking for my Normal details. It was as if nothing had ever happened. Nobody, including my best friends, knew anything. But they knew about the devils and knew too that somehow P had been awful. They had hated him instantly, with the loyalty of all Best Friends.

'It's okay. He isn't here.'

'And he never will be.'

'You don't have to write back.'

I was so used to being a good girl that until then, I did not know that I had this option. Moved with so much support from my friends and blinded with tears, I mustered up the courage to be bad enough to tear the letter into the tiniest pieces I could. I'd never reply because I had never received it. Wasn't the post marvellous!

There was no dustbin around. The closest possibility was a huge crack (leading to a huge hole) in the cement parapet by the teachers' cottage. I shoved all the pieces neatly inside, pushing them so tight that even the wind couldn't blow them away.

A few days later, we were once again sitting at the same spot. 'What is that!' my friends screamed, amused and scared at the same time. I jumped! 'That' was a little rock that moved. A true toad watching us with his true toad eyes. Next to the hole, holding pieces of an unloved letter (which were still there!). From then onwards, every evening, the toad appeared.

'Ritu's pet toad.'

'Ritu, you should kiss it.'

'Yes. Then it will be Ritu's pet prince.'

My trash had been recycled into a sort of insulation lining, a blanket with breathing space, for the toad's house to keep him warm in the cold nights. Evening after evening, the grateful toad greeted us, content to squat quietly beside us. Though I never touched him, he had indeed become a pet. He never came out during school hours or when others were present. He never stopped visiting. We did. I wish I'd been as loyal to him as he'd been to us.

In our short time together, the nameless toad taught me to be kind to the ugly, the unwanted, the unseen. People like myself. One late afternoon, after study time, the girls ran down the flights of stairs with the joy and freedom of soldiers returning home after battle. As always, I was slow, observing everything and everyone. On one of the cool mosaic-tiled steps was a chubby, grotesque gecko, lying on its back. Feet after feet jumped joyfully over its exposed tummy, blissfully unaware that they were murdering him. It tried in vain to roll itself on its back and run away. Here was the animal I was the most terrified of! Somehow, I managed to summon the courage to extend my keds-clad toe towards him, holding my breath for the few eternal seconds of torture, and finally was able to tip him up on his side as gently as I could. It was just the perfect pressure he needed to roll around, which he did. Promptly! And wiggled away thanklessly, running as fast as only a gecko in danger can.

Important Lesson No. 18: Own Power means helping others in spite of Own Fears.

One afternoon, on the terrace where we washed and hung our socks and underwear to dry, I heard a mysteriously soft squeak. It came not from a door or a dark corner but from an iron bucket in the middle of the terrace. I went to investigate. In there, clawing helplessly against the slippery smooth inner walls of the bucket to avoid drowning in the small puddle of water inside, was a rat! A disgusting, scary, furry grey rat with a creepy rat's tail. Yet it was impossible to not feel bad for the vile creature. There was no way I was going to touch it. Should I empty the water out? What if it leaped out on me? Or worse still, bit me? Yikes, I couldn't have it touch me! I looked around and found a white plastic bag. I twisted it and folded it over itself for added strength. Then, I slung it like a rope into a well. The intelligent mouse understood instantly! It grabbed the plastic bag and I pulled it out onto the floor. It shivered, coughed and then disappeared in a blink!

Sister Carmella, a hip, young, new principal arrived, giving our school fresh peppermint breath. She:

1. Openly admired my bookworm ways.
2. Christened me Walking Encyclopaedia (instantly making the whole school slightly in awe of me).
3. Said hello to me all the time.

One night, several of us Periwinklers were saying goodbye to our friends in the upper dorms where they had gathered to drink water. Silence was expected, for it was bedtime after all. But it was never strictly enforced (perhaps because it was just a matter of a few minutes, perhaps because it was the end of another long, tiring day). Out of nowhere, Sister Carmella appeared and hit my happy cheek (swollen with smiles while waving to Noor and Diya upstairs) so loudly that not only did it sting my being, but it also stunned into silence the groups of giggling girls on both floors. Everyone walked away with feelings of pity and relief that it had not been them. I held my burning cheek, now wet with scalding tears of shame, shocked.

Important Lesson No. 19: Grown-ups can never be your friends.

P, M or Sister Carmella were grown-ups and all of them used their power to oppress, betray, humiliate and hurt us for only one reason — because they could. They used their power to abuse us in ways that were inconsequential to them, but huge to us. Emotional abuse is the worst of all, for it leaves no scars, but hurts for years. Children have no choice. Sometimes we even love our oppressors because they are all we know. But growing up was beginning to change that. Unknown to us then, we were slowly learning to hate bitterly and and to understand the power it held — the power of bitterness. (Of course, it would take decades to realize that this power was like a mirage. Real Power was something else altogether, something these grown-ups had no idea about. Something I was beginning to discover as Own Power.)

The party in sixth grade ended soon. Burdened with funding three households, Pup-Pa could no longer afford to pay my boarding school fees. His responsibilities stuck on him as fat, making him round, like a watermelon — and just as fragile, threatening to burst into a bloody mess at the merest trigger. Unknown to me, my two-in-one status as *Maahaara* and a Moral Science topper had melted the heart of the new Sister Superior, who was a factory of Vitamin K. She generously offered to pay a huge chunk of my school fees, and so I remained in boarding. But I was still a child and it didn't strike me that this would impact my extracurriculars. I had signed up for guitar classes, not knowing that it cost extra money. Another nun said furiously, 'Shame on you!' It took me a while to put two and two together and when I did, it felt like somebody had spat in my face. I swallowed the shame right away, without question, like children tend to do.

Shame had managed to wipe out the joy of music in me. Still, there was the relief of dodging dodgeball legally, without the nagging anxiety of being discovered. The guitar teacher was a short, blind old man from Darjeeling. His stout shoulders stood out like puffed sleeves. His faded checkered shirts had lived for a long, long time like their wearer. But we couldn't tell his age. Movies had taught us that the visually impaired:

1. Always wore heavy, black sunglasses.
2. Always carried a cane.
3. They were very sensitive.
4. They were very sweet and kind.
5. And they often played music.

He matched the description to a T. It was natural to feel a surge of love and respect for him. When he left, we'd watch his back in awe, seeing how he manoeuvred the steep slopes and steps so effortlessly with only his frail stick for guidance. I tried to imitate him a few times. Once, I grabbed a stick near a tree, closed my eyes and tried walking down the tiny flight of cement steps near the primary section. Almost instantly, I toppled. Another time, I spread out my bare hands in front of me, rudders in the air, walking in a plain area (plain enough for us to assemble in on school mornings). I fared much better on this forgiving surface, managing to go on for almost two minutes before bumping gently into a tiny parapet which marked the boundary of the garden. There was so much freedom in walking around like this, shutting out the world. I envied Guitar Sir and all the blind people of the world. Until then, I had not realized just how much stimulation is constantly thrown at us, even if the vision ahead is something pleasant like trees. And just how tiring it is to process this constant stream of information. Blind people could simply tune out this continuous stimulation.

At guitar class, I wanted to learn the chords and know their notes like I did my peepul. But the teacher catered to popular demand and directly taught us songs we could perform. There was no time for details. One day, while he tuned the guitar, he put his hand on my lap, high up my thigh, but not too high. My heart leaped into my throat and lay captive there along with my breath. (Not again!) I dropped my guitar in shock. It dropped on his shoe and rolled over, unscathed. Apparently, I had not been singled out. Other girls revealed this had happened to them too. Was it because he was blind? And so, he was feeling his way across the world as usual? Or was it because he was a man? Were all men like this? I didn't care to find out. I hated him, instantly, yet felt sorry (and I'm ashamed to admit, still some affection) for him. It was too much confusion to swim in while dealing with childhood. I couldn't learn music while fighting off panic attacks. I gave up guitar lessons.

'You are a selfish, flighty, ungrateful and undeserving girl,' admonished the same nun, right in my face. Pup-Pa was informed promptly. A rare trunk call followed during which he threw a fit. 'We are living on charity and here you are with your expensive whims. And then abandoning them!' I listened quietly, not daring to tell him how in spite of all the shame, I still loved music as much as any child. I didn't dare tell him about my brief stint (free because a nun taught it) in piano last year, which I had actually abandoned even though I loved it. Why? Because a kid had told me that only Catholic girls are allowed to play the piano beyond the fifth grade. I had obeyed without questioning her (once again where obedience wasn't necessary) or even doubting it to be true. It took me a whole year to find out that this was totally untrue. I simply had to ask (like one asks for help) and I could have just continued to play piano. And this guitar episode would never have happened. (I did not know then that I would not play a musical instrument again for three decades.)

Again, my evenings were about trying to hide. Sometimes, I was lucky. On other days, I had to show up at dodgeball. When asked about my whereabouts, my lies ranged from:

1. Being in the bathroom.
2. Finishing my homework.
3. Meeting my local guardian.
4. Simply being unaware of the time because I was praying in the chapel.
5. I was crying for my late mother.

The last two always worked like a charm, enough to evoke Vitamin K-induced approval. Some days, I would hang around the cages of the partridges and rabbits that Sister Celestine took care of. Rumour had it that she was close to 100 years. Time had dwarfed her, turned her eyes almost liquid, gifted her a hunchback and painted her face with wrinkles, which made it impossible to tell what she was thinking. She also took care of a parrot as unimaginative as his name, Mitthu, the name of every second parakeet in the country. He was a big fightercock. I avoided him. I never did get along with parakeets. On other days, I hid by the pigsty at the far end of the campus, which was full of cute, fat pigs. Behind it lay the graveyard. I couldn't help wondering if the pigs ever partied with ghosts and exchanged stories.

Being around animals was divine because:

1. You never felt alone.
2. You never had to put up a performance. Around people, you always had to put on performances.

> An endless series of performances. That's why humans were so exhausting! Animals and my peepul were not.

During one of those hideaways, I saw one of the biggest of all the Big Girls calling out to the rest of her classmates. The scattered tenth graders somehow gathered together and headed towards the square, walking up the stairs and into the auditorium upstairs. I had a second to make a choice before I was discovered. I could either go on trying to hide or go dodge balls instead of bad luck. Or I could try something new (which clearly did not involve sports) and sneak in with the Big Girls. I ran up, being the last in the crowd of girls, settling easily into the forgiving darkness of the auditorium. It had been especially darkened for a screening of some sort. Today was my lucky day.

A fat, short, middle-aged nun with a grim face was making large gestures with her hands, one of which held a white pen that glowed brightly in the blackness. She stood near a brightly lit screen, which was blank for now, but emitted enough light for us to see her clearly. A huge pair of spectacles covered most of her face. A huge wart with hair growing from its centre, covered a great deal of what remained. I had never seen her before on campus. Who was she?

'Hello, girls. I am Sister Maria,' she said.

What was she doing here?

'I am a counsellor. And I am here to teach you something very important about you.'

What could be so important about us? Our bodies?

'Your bodies.' The telepathy was spooking me out! '...Your bodies as women.'

She proceeded to show some diagrams on the screen of red, pink and blue tubes of what she called the Female Reproductive System. Complaining whispers sounded from everywhere.

'What a bore!'

'We were taught this years ago!'

'Can't believe we had to miss basketball for this.'

'These nuns!'

The nun's droning combined with the collective whining around produced a very soothing noise. I didn't realize I had fallen asleep until I woke up groggy and aware of a lapse of time as soon as I saw the screen — now filled with a ghastly photograph. In plain plastic buckets were small human limbs. 'This is saltwater abortion. A salt water injection flushes out the baby's parts. See how the babies get burned before they're killed.' Wait, so those were burnt hands and legs of foetuses! Was I awake? What was dream? What was reality?

'Even once if a man's penis penetrates. Even once and you could get pregnant. And do you really want this?'

'...God created you holy. Keep yourself holy until it is time...'

It had taken me years to figure out that the feelings of disgust born in P's house which had followed me everywhere ever since, were those of Shame. But now I knew the reason why. I was unholy. That's why being in this body felt uncomfortable so often. Athletics, dance, sport, otherwise innocent and popular joys involved the body playing. But mine was vile, so no wonder I didn't enjoy any of these. In that moment of enlightenment, I was instantly grateful and depressed beyond words. Still these feelings were luxuries now that I knew where babies came from. I had been penetrated. Forget vile, I was pregnant! Oh my god!

Oh my god! Oh my god! Oh my god!

What was I going to do? It was clearly too late, so maybe I'd need a saltwater abortion and birthe the corpse of a baby, one charred part after another. No, I couldn't do that!

I wished I had spared myself this horror and not sneaked into the auditorium. I wished that like other children, I too, had found out in stages where babies come from:

1. From storks and Heaven.
2. From an orphanage.
3. From a sperm.
4. From a sperm which is inside a woman. It has a tail. The tail fattens up and a baby is born.
5. It only takes nine months. If it's longer, then No Baby.

I wish I had known the last part. The Most Important! I wish I had someone to talk to. Someone safe.

For what seemed like an eternity, I lived through a continuous panic attack, silent and invisible to all around me. There were many joys in my life. I had never felt more protected. I finally had friends. Even a pet toad! But none of it mattered as I starred in my own horror documentary.

Abuse and its side effects stay with you, flowing through you like a gritty river full of sharp stones. You don't know when you'll be pricked and where, often for seemingly unrelated, completely mundane and even circumstances that are absolutely fine. I tried and tried but could not convince the five-year-old still trapped within me that the horrors were in the past. She refused to believe that I was now (more or less) safe (even if I was pregnant). She found reality so unbearable that she refused to want to look at it.

The Tentacle now gave me conjunctivitis. My eyes inflamed with anger, hurt and resentment and had to be forced open. Thick, gooey yellow tears fell by themselves. Conjunctivitis meant a brief respite from the routine, lines, uniforms, games time, etcetera. It also meant some time with other infected girls, which included the biggest of the Big Girls.

I approached a tenth grader in dark sunglasses like Guitar Sir's, but far more stylish. 'Hi didi. Can I ask you something?' She looked at me with the maternal instinct Big Girls naturally had when younger ones approached them hesitantly. It made them feel important and truly big.

'Of course, anything!' she said gently.

'It's not... um... appropriate. And I'm... um... sorry... um... I don't know how to... Or who else to ask. But I simply must... um... know. It isn't about curiosity... it's a matter of life and death. It's a friend. She... I mean I, I mean she...

'It's okay. What's wrong?'

'How do you know you're carrying a baby?' I asked.

Shocked into laughter, yet sweet enough to not judge, she said, 'Well, you don't get your period.'

'What do you mean? We always have school and school is full of periods.'

'Huh! No, not that! Hahaha!'

'Don't you know what a period is?' she asked, trying to hide her amusement.

I shook my head. 'Only the school ones. I hate games period.'

'Well, you'll have one anytime now. So you had better know.'

'So there's this uterus here,' she said, pointing to the area below her belly button. 'And it prepares for a baby. And if it doesn't happen, then a lot of blood comes out. And this is Normal. Every month, a lot of blood and tissue and muscle.'

I nodded, proud to be considered big enough to consume such Important Facts.

'So, if it doesn't happen, then you're not pregnant?'

'No. To be pregnant, you have to first be able to have a period. If not, then you can't be pregnant.'

'Even if you're not holy?'

She looked at me strangely. Perhaps she understood everything that I had not said. Perhaps I imagined she did.

'Your friend is not pregnant.'

I ran, crying. No Baby Tears. Tears of Relief.

My eyes healed.

Once again, a stranger had changed my life.

Whenever we passed each other, we said simple hellos, as if we'd never had an intimate conversation. I was ashamed and deeply grateful — a two-in-one paradox that would be my house for many years.

My horror film ended. But somewhere along the way, something I couldn't name shut down in me. Perhaps it was childhood. The feelings of my younger selves who, along with the Tentacle, lived in me in bits. Abandonment, anger and shame became a silent mountain of bitterness. Something had to erupt. It did soon enough, in the most visible way.

A strange illness silently took over the boarding school. In Periwinkle, I saw it manifest as fever, crankiness and rashes, which led to the sick children being quarantined out of sight in the Sick Room. Midterm exams were on when Valini began to show the symptoms. Aunty Amelia had her bed moved to the corner, right next to her curtained paradise, isolating her from the rest of us. We were not to touch the sick ones or even talk to them. While we crammed our brains with study, most of it stuff that would prove to be useless very soon, and then entertained ourselves with idle chatter, Valini sat alone in her solitary confinement on her bed, watching us from a distance. She only had to wait a day until preparations were made for her to shift to the Sick Room. Yet, every second spent alone sitting on your bed with nothing to entertain you, no permission to move, unless you had to go to the bathroom, and that too, supervised, was torture, even for an 11-year-old. One day could feel like a month of solitary confinement. She tried calling out to her 'friends', but everybody ignored her. 'I'm not an Untouchable, you know!' she screamed in desperation, finally. 'What a thing to say, Valini! We're just trying to keep you and the rest of the girls safe,' said Aunty Amelia.

In Valini's outburst, I recognized the deep loneliness, the walls of anger due to the lack of connection — things that were a way of life for the wounded child in me. The awful feeling of invisibility often forced upon me/her for the convenience of others. The consequent rage of not even being acknowledged. I had to help her! When everybody left for evening tea, I reached out to her, held her hand, looking back to ensure that I remained undiscovered. 'You are not an Untouchable,' I said to her. 'Nobody should be one.' Into her hands, I placed my favourite *20,000 Leagues Under The Sea* as well as a couple of Tinkles, probably a closer match to her sensibilities. 'Here, you can borrow these. Disinfect them in the sun and return when you're done. There is no rush. I've read them quite a few times already.' She gave me a Cheshire Cat smile. I patted her hand and ran off before Aunty Amelia could catch me or a Tattlecock reported me. My heart leapt in joy as I beamed with the two-in-one thrill of having done a random act of kindness, which was also illegal.

I was certain that the grown-ups were overreacting as usual and that a few seconds of helping somebody would not infect me. However, hours later at bedtime, I felt sluggish and weak like one does with fever and saw the first sneaky rash appear on my foot. Damn! I knew I had to report myself right away. But I didn't. The next morning was the very last paper, maths. I had studied very hard and didn't want to miss it and then have to repeat it later once I had recovered. I simply had to hold on for a few hours more. How hard could that be? Very, I discovered soon enough. The disease was spreading at the speed of a flooded gutter, filling me with its filth. I downed half of the new bottle of Dexorange Iron Tonic (which Pup-Pa had given me and which I otherwise used as a midnight snack if I was hungry), hoping its superpowers would at least keep the bugs on hold until I had finished writing my maths paper. No such luck! I had to muster all of my mental strength to get through that morning, put up a performance of normalcy so I wasn't found out, and somehow finish the paper. I could barely make sense of anything. The digits in the question paper danced and blurred. At least, I'd pass. As I handed in my paper to the supervising teacher, I exhaled out the facade. I didn't need to say anything. She held my arm, called in a substitute and took me to the Boarding. A nun collected me like a parcel, passing me on to Aunty Amelia who deposited me in Valini's bed (which is how I discovered that it wasn't Valini's bed). It was the Bed of Shame. Like a park bench, anybody could be on it. The girls returned. Some stared at me and whispered into each other's ears with cupped hands, ensuring their secrets didn't leak out. But their scornful eyes and laughter gave them away. For that afternoon, I was the joke of Periwinkle, the open subject of shame. The stupid girl who had contracted chicken pox on purpose.

Fortunately, my torture didn't last long. Thanks to Valini, arrangements had been made for spontaneous cases and I was shifted into the Sick Room within a couple of hours.

In spite of its dreary name, the Sick Room wasn't dreary at all. It was spacious, bursting with light and pink beds — many of them wonderfully empty, so I could choose the one I wanted. No uniforms here, no rules and no lines! Half a dozen girls floated around here in white cotton chemises brought from home and usually worn under uniforms. Each one was joyfully different, revealing stories — stories of individuality that we were unaware of. Like who had bought these, where were they from. And what they said about the wearer. Mine was a clingy one with skinny spaghetti straps, the length of a mini skirt. It stood out from the other knee-length frock ones with generous skirting.

'That's sexy,' said an eighth grader.

A new word. Illegal-sounding.

'What does it mean?'

'Boys will like them.'

'Oh!' I said instinctively, pulling it down to cover as much more of me as possible.

'Don't worry. They are not here!' she laughed.

I laughed nervously, carefully hiding what the Tentacle might reveal and why I wanted to attract zero attention from men ever. The elegant buttercup yellow bra straps on her skinny shoulders, peeking out from under her chemise, told me how different our worlds were. Each grade was as different as a planet. Multiple grade differences meant being in different universes altogether!

'Thank God! Right? I mean, look at us. We're covered in boils which are covered in powder. No one wants to see us like that.'

'Right!'

Why was it so necessary to agree? Why was it so necessary to seek approval? Even in the most unnecessary of circumstances? My zero self-worth wouldn't know other options for many years. And I'd mistake fleeting approval for the Feeling of Love.

The weeks spent in the Sick Room were calm, full of space and laughter. Food was brought to us. Endless slices of watermelon were served to us. Being sick was so much fun, with so much freedom. I never wanted to leave. I lay on top of my bunk bed (we never had bunk beds otherwise!) by the window, reading for hours. The oldest, a tenth grader, was wearing a nightie that gave her the appearance of an aunty, a role she played by becoming a mother hen to all of us. If there were any fights (like the time when the real winner of my UNO cards game was me and not Valini), she'd break us up. She'd save the best watermelon slices for us. She'd ensure that visits of people like Meana Didi (who often delivered medicines, food and sundries to us) were short and sweet. She'd ensure that each of the bras washed and hung didn't overlap and got equal drying rights. Smriti Singh should have been there to know the true meaning of being a minder. I wished I had an aunty like that back home. Or at least an older sister. The softness, the effortless love a maternal figure brings could be healing like chilled rose sherbet on a scorching day.

In the Sick Room, we also discovered the multiple talents of toothpaste! We used it to make beautiful patterns on empty rinds of watermelon. We played gentle Holi by spraying multicoloured toothpastes and talcum powders onto each other. All was wonderful until the rains arrived. In the mountains, monsoon acquires a primal ferocity bringing with it landslides, boisterous noises and at nightfall, the real fear of ghosts. At night, the torrential downpours created a deafening percussion interrupted by the rhythmic taps of the *chowkidar's* lathi as he went about his rounds. Sleep was impossible. We began to swear that the drumbeats were interrupted by the occasional jingling sounds of anklets. This eerie concert made us see what we always saw but never realized. The graveyard! Below the Sick Room lay a cemented path and the pigsty and beyond it in plain view, numerous graves in a wild garden of weeds. There was no woman in sight at that hour. All the ingredients of a B-grade movie — wild rains, an ancient watchman on his nightly rounds, mountains and vulnerable spectators — were present. This couldn't be real life. However, a survey conducted the next morning concluded that all participants had heard the *chan chan* of the anklets. So it had to be real. Reality was now spookier than a cheap horror film.

I wrote about all of this in a handwritten letter, promptly disinfected in the sun, and delivered via the tenth-grader to Meana Didi, who (surprise, surprise!) actually had a heart. The letter did reach my father! But he dismissed it as a simple fever and unlike the other parents of the infected children, never came to get me. 'Still, this lack of love and care is better than the special care at P's house when you had measles,' said Voice of Reason. P and his successors' shadows somehow hung around in my life, living a parallel life inside me in brackets, darkening everything in bits and pieces.

Sadly, my rashes healed very soon, cutting my holiday short. I returned with my tattoo-like scars, some of which would last a lifetime, to Periwinkle, school, rules, lines, uniforms... the mundane world of the healthy.

Behind my back, the girls had all learned to knit, keeping lovely woollies ready for grading. I was jittery. Where would I learn knitting now? Mala, a girl from Dimples, discussed this with Mrs Kipling, who turned out to be a knitting saviour! Within a week, I had a lovely chocolate brown muffler in my name, ready to be exhibited and graded. When I said it looked too masculine and that I'd prefer a headscarf instead, for practical purposes, Mrs Kipling didn't question a child's tantrum or shame her for apparent ingratitude. Instead, she quickly added short strips to it, magically transforming the muffler into a head scarf. In a stormy life, the generosity of strangers like her are like rainbows brightening the sky.

Letitia was an Anglo-Indian girl who sat on the back-most bench in the classroom's darkest corner. A sweet-natured girl, she always smiled when spoken to, and spoke only what was necessary. Her sadness was evident in her desperate need for invisibility. Yet she stood out, perhaps because of her big size. Having consistently failed sixth grade for several years, Letitia was much older than us. Our common lack of self-worth should have made us friends, creating history with a friendship between a backbencher and a first-bencher. But somehow, we didn't find each other.

Soon, Diwali holidays dawned upon us. The four-day break was like rain in a desertscape for all children of course, but even more so, for their parents. Pup-Pa, too busy saving the world, obviously wasn't one of them. Only about two dozen of us remained, making the campus appear even more enormous and empty, revealing just how parched it was for love. We stuck to the central area where I had once impressed a principal enough to have gotten admission and where I had walked pretending to be blind. In spite of the heavy wind, the sisters had decked up the entire area with clay lamps. The flames flickered, went comatose and died randomly, but were always brought back to life by a passing didi or sister. It was the most beautiful night, as if the stars themselves had descended on earth to rest and have a picnic in the hills.

On Diwali night, when it was late, way past our bedtime, we collected in the playground. The nuns loved us in their own way. They had kindly given us firecrackers and special meals. So we didn't feel forsaken like leftovers on the night of the country's most loved festival. The magic of gunpowder lit up the playground, the delight of the children somehow overtaking the noise of the firecrackers. Rockets, sparklers, electric pencils and wires and my favourite *anars* (what I called flowerpots), snakes and *chakris* (or spinning wheels) put us under their spell. It was all pretty and peaceful, till somebody found a *laddoo*-like thing called a Laxmi atom bomb. We simply had to burst it, but it was missing a wick. An idea struck me. 'We could wrap up the thing in paper, twist a long end into a long tail that could double up for a wick, which we could then light safely,' I said.

'Genius!' said one of the girls. 'But, where will we get paper from?' asked another. Their faces fell, excitement fizzling out of them like spoilt crackers refusing to ignite. 'Wait!' I said. They looked up in surprise. 'I have notebooks in my locker. I can tear a double sheet from the centerfold to give us extra space.' Their faces lit up. They jumped in delight like the rocket cracker we had just launched. 'Go! Go fast,' said one. 'And come back fast,' said another.

I ran up the giant cement stairs as fast as I could towards the basement near Periwinkle where the lockers were. Since all of us were away in the playground, only that area was lit up. Barring the central lights of the basement and the restrooms beyond, it was pitch dark. It took my eyes a few seconds to get used to the darkness. That's when I saw a shadowy muscular figure, as black as the night itself. It was moving slowly, very slowly, as if in a hypnotic dance. Something about It resembled the grace of a cat. How had It scaled up the lockers? How could It have claws that didn't slip against the slippery smooth metal locker walls? Did It place Its claws in the gaps between the lockers for a grip? The gaps were made up with mathematical precision, you had to know how to multiply to figure them out. Was It intelligent enough to know multiplication tables? Was It a math genius? Was I hallucinating? I rubbed my eyes vigorously, adjusting them to the dim light. The creature turned around to glare at me with Its mean, piercing eyes, which pierced through the Tentacle. In the blackness of Its body merging with the absolute blackness of the night, Its eyes burned like fire. The reason It resembled the grace of a cat was because It *was* a cat! A big cat! It leapt towards me, a leap big enough to look like it was flying. Turning around, I ran as fast as I could! So fast that I could no longer feel my legs on the rocky mountain ground. Like the big cat, I too, was flying. My chest burned in agony as my screaming WholeHeartWithaHole ordered that I stop running this very second! I returned to Earth, my feet spinning mechanically like bicycle wheels. Hitting something, a rock perhaps, I fell... rolling and rolling and rolling down the slope into nothingness. All I remember are the emerald eyes burning like *diya* flames, staring straight into mine and my heart ablaze in pain.

When I came to, I discovered my knees were bleeding. There were scrapes on my elbows, arms and shins. I got up, dusted my body and took a few deep breaths. I was at the other end (or the beginning) of the campus, almost at the school gate. The panther was nowhere in sight. I was grateful that I had read *The Jungle Book* and encyclopaedias to know what the mysterious creature was.

I had definitely met a panther! That wasn't imagined. But my wounds weren't deep enough to have been created by jaws and claws. Was it like Bagheera? Or did it flee in fright?

Something was different about me. I touched my neck, arms and legs. Was I still me? My automatic steps to the basement were as unsure and unsteady as I was. In a daze, as if possessed by the spirit of the panther, I opened my locker, pulled out my notebook, tore the double sheet from the centerfold, closed my locker and mechanically walked back to the others waiting in the playground. The soft flames all around now irked me. The unforgettable brightness of the big panther's eyes had been tattooed into my memory. In a flash, I knew why. If you took away their brilliance, they were similar to P's cruel, dull, snot-coloured eyes. It was why I hated cats and all things feline-eyed. The beast I had somehow miraculously escaped wasn't so horrific itself as its eyes were. Something faintly resembling a warrior's spirit rose up inside me, with intense smouldering anger, making me want to murder P, the panther, and myself. Flaming tears flowed down my face, burning the paths they travelled upon. That is how I became aware of the scratches on my face.

'Rittu, where are you?' said one girl.

'What's wrong? You look different,' said another.

'I'm not feeling too well. I'll just sit down for a bit,' I said, heading towards the giant steps. A bursting flowerpot's glare lit us up, revealing my wounds.

'Hey, what happened to you?'

'Oh my God! Are you okay?'

'Nothing. Just minor scratches. I had a fall,' I said. 'Don't worry, I have Boroline. No need to take me to the dispensary.'

'Are you sure? Let's get you to the dispensary, anyway.'

'Of course! No, no! Nothing that Boroline can't fix. Just let me rest, okay?'

'Alright!'

'Look, let's wrap this up.'

'And twist the tail. Don't forget that.'

Many pairs of hands went up to their ears in defence as the bomb exploded, deafening us briefly. All I heard was silence. That's when it struck me. I had just had another NDE. My second near-death experience.

For the next few days, I found myself gagging in disgust in the dining hall. Being able to keep a cup of beige milk down was itself always a Herculean task. The food too, was mostly gag-worthy, especially the *gatte ki subzi*. The cooks had this unique talent of somehow transforming this beloved Rajasthani delicacy into something with rock-hard dumplings that even the pigs at the pigsty (who'd eat anything!) sniffed and moved away from immediately, snorting in disgust. But now my body was shutting out even animal products like eggs, chicken and meat which I'd always loved.

A panther forced me to go vegetarian! This shift in diet was something that would last till my late teens. The panther gave gifts far greater than the ones it took away. It gave me a voice. Overnight, I began to sing. And write, mostly poetry and songs. Both gifts moved the hundreds of girls, nuns, teachers, and everyone at school. They consumed, transformed beyond themselves, wanting more and more. I delivered, from somewhere beyond myself. Not knowing then that this was what art did, what art was always supposed to do. It put us in touch with our essence, which lay beyond identities.

The panther's stealth lived on in a recurring dream, which would creep up on me for many nights. The same gorgeous green hills, its peaks hidden here and there in the clouds. Hundreds of papers floating in mid-air, keeping the mist company. The lake in the centre was still a mirror to everything. The clouds, the forest, the pages. But this time, something rose from its waters without creating a ripple. Several dream recordings revealed what was surging up. A huge, purple-blue-gold bird, unlike any I had ever seen! One dawn, I realized that this was no ordinary creature. Its eyes were the same colour as Maa's name — Ruby. It was a phoenix! The mythical bird of rebirth, with one difference. Instead of rising from the ashes, this firebird was rising from the water.

12

Langur Fest

Unlike most children, I was grateful for a boring and solitary winter break. (Almost) no people meant (almost) no performances. What freedom! Things had been quiet till Christmas Eve, when Pup-Pa was away on a night shift to ensure the tracks were healthy on his route, so the big trains could make it safely to the big city (Bombay). I was left with the D'Souzas. He thought I'd be delighted because they had two children, just a few years older than I. I was happy that he was happy. He was happy because he thought I was happy. And so went the countless cycles of invisible responsibilities that both parents and children bear, most of them completely unnecessary, but of course, we only discover their futility in the luxury of hindsight.

At midnight, we were on the pews down on our knees for the only Midnight Mass I have ever attended. While Vapi slept, a hundred or so of its people dressed in their finest, shiniest things quietly flocked together in the silent night, from the many different directions of the small town to collect at the little church for Midnight Mass. At the pews, winter sweat trickled down my legs. Unknown to me, it copulated with oxygen to turn all that it touched into maroon.

The Mass finished. Christmas was declared. Seriousness swam away. That special joy, which is the signature of all festivals, rained in, beaming through our joyful faces. We crossed the railway tracks once again to return to the D'Souzas's home. The fluorescent tube lights turned on, enlightening me that this sweat had colour. My eyes followed their zigzag trails. So red that they had tie-dyed my socks and the skirt of my beautiful ivory organza party frock into a shade which almost matched its crimson velvet bodice. Aunty and her daughter saw this as I ran to the bathroom. My chipmunk panties bravely held as much blood as they could. But like the bodies of dead soldiers on a battlefield, they now had to be discarded. Grateful (for once!) for a woman in the house, I ran to D'Souza Aunty asking for help. She stared through me as if I were a lizard on a faraway wall, saying nothing until she finally walked away. Grown-ups, especially those who were used to being treated like they were invisible themselves, had a way of making children feel even more unseen. (Not Own Power.) Having seen this in so many aunties, I was used to this. I went back to the bathroom, cleaned myself, bathed and changed. The organza material of my frock had absorbed everything like a sponge. No more blood poured out of me. On Christmas day, everyone poured port endlessly. The few wild drops that had gone astray on the white tablecloth looked so much like what, I did not know then, had been my first period.

In the new year, everything was truly new, covering the still vacant spots on the weirdness spectrum. Over a series of scattered and unrelated inland letters and trunk calls, Pup-Pa and MultipleSources informed me that I now had a baby sister. How strange! I knew far more about the Cheshire Cat, Caterpillar and Captain Nemo than I did about my own sibling. Diya left the school. Noor found new friends who were far less gloomy. My toad stayed. Just when I was beginning to find my academic rhythm once again, seventh grade threw brand new subjects into our faces like Holi colours. Like the powders themselves, the subjects — history, civics, geography and the trio that science had split into — stung our eyes and tainted our skin. We had a choice between Gujarati and Sanskrit, two-in-one languages which were simultaneously both Indian and foreign. Being a bookworm, teachers' pet, a non-Gujarati and more, it seemed obvious that I'd pick the more intellectually fashionable one. But I lived in Gujarat, where Gujarati was spoken and would therefore, be useful. Nobody saw that I had chosen life over death, a living language over a dead one. Pup-Pa was mortified and furious. The grown-ups who had been on my side, till then, were all embarrassed. Noor had chosen Sanskrit too. Learning a foreign-Indian language became an unnecessarily lonely affair.

Computer science became a huge deal overnight, big enough to merit two teachers. One spat out hate at us non-stop, while the other quieter one, seemed to live, walk and breathe in a shell. Both showed us less empathy than a robot might have. And we (well, definitely I), needed empathy in large doses because nothing was making any sense anywhere, anymore.

Back at Boarding, I had shifted to Buds, a tiny dorm in the Big Girls' wing, housing fewer than two dozen chosen ones. We had to face a loving, highly eccentric matron whose reign went well beyond Buds, into every corner of every dorm and every bathroom in the Big Girls' world. Small, hunching over herself so much that in a decade she might have curled herself into a ball, she walked the corridors, often with a ruler in her iron hand. It was more for effect because she never used it, preferring other, more colourful forms of punishment. One afternoon, a few of the bigger Big Girls were playing catch across their beds with a sealed packet of Whisper. Packets of sanitary napkins were given to the girls who needed them, wrapped in newspaper, concealed in Shame. Such hypocrisy! That too, in an all-female world. Everybody could immediately tell what those newspaper-wrapped packages were. By being defiant and shunning unsaid and unnecessary rules of modesty, these Big Girls were being warriors. Sister Louise wafted in, catching the Whisper in mid-air, taking it away with her, leaving the girls to fend for themselves in the midst of their period. A Forfeit! (That's what such punishments were called. I never heard it being used outside of my boarding school.) I'm not sure if they apologized well enough and were forgiven or whether they collected solitary pads as alms from others.

As young ladies, we were expected to not 'tempt' (a word that was becoming a favourite of the nuns) the young *dhobi* by hand-washing our own undergarments and socks, then hanging them to dry on the terrace.

Many did not pick up their clothes for days after they had dried. Sister Louise would then have Nanhi Didi (a sweet, gossipy middle-aged lady) lay them out on an empty extra bed. If they were still not picked up, she'd have Nanhi Didi place the bras and panties, with the aid of a tall stick, on the wings of the most centrally located ceiling fans in the dorm. The fans would be turned on, the speed depending on her temper's temperature. Humble bras and cotton panties would then fly in all directions, landing on beds, heads and lockers. The owners of these beds, heads and lockers the bras and panties landed on had to keep them whether or not these belonged to them. In case the underclothes landed on NoMan'sLand, then whoever's beds, heads and lockers were the closest, had to keep the treasures. Everyone would look sufficiently ashamed — but only till Sister Louise, some well-known Tattlecocks and Nanhi Didi were out of sight. Immediately afterwards, raucous and uncontrollable laughter would flood the dorms.

This routine was only for unmarked underwear. If even a faintly legible marking of a boarding school number remained, then brutal punishment awaited us. The owners were first called out sweetly by their numbers. They would then have to kneel down by that same extra bed. Sister Louise would finally use her ruler not to hit, but as a tool to pick up the undergarments which she'd then place unceremoniously onto the heads of their respective owners. God help them if there were too many to fit on one small head! All criminals thus, sought god's forgiveness by saying a favourite prayer.

Our Father who art in Heaven
Hallowed be thy name
Thy kingdom come
Thy will be done
on Earth, as it is in Heaven.
Give us this day our daily bread
And forgive us our trespasses
as we forgive those who trespass against us.
And lead us not into temptation
But deliver us from evil.

For thine is the kingdom
The power and the glory
For ever and ever.
Amen.

In the absence of any anchors, all of this newness was terribly scary. The familiar fills one with comfort, which is why change, or the unknown, is always freaky. (Years later, I'd discover that it wasn't the unknown or the change itself but our definition and expectations of the unknown and the change which was scary.) This was also probably the reason why I found myself drawn deeper and deeper into self-reflection and it explains my first trysts with the metaphysical. I discovered Buddhism first in textbooks, then in information I hunted down in whatever text I could find in a predominantly Catholic environment, devouring it in the chapel during the quiet siesta hours.

The cool chapel and its soothing refuge were now even closer than ever before! Behind Buds was an entry to the chapel, private enough to be accessed even in one's nightgown. In the tiny space between the chapel and Buds, I discovered a slightly hollow tile. Kneeling, I tried to pull it open, hoping to find treasures older than the Angelus bell. It opened easily, revealing a small, neat, dust-free room. A generous window ensured it was well lit. Clearly, it was well maintained and regularly visited. I had found the perfect hiding space! Now I only had to find the perfect non-visiting hours to be alone here.

I learned about Buddhism's Four Noble Truths, becoming an encyclopaedia on suffering. I vowed to devote my life to the eightfold path, especially the Middle Path. I openly declared that I was now a Buddhist and must not be called Hindu. Amused, people around me gave me 'okay' stares before moving on to other matters. My relationship with Mama Mary stayed intact.

Determined to regain lost ground in my studies, I avoided the games period to sneak in some extra study time. I had discovered a spot where nobody went to after school. Behind the playground was a row of toilets, and right behind them a corridor and cool mosaic stairs which led up to a balcony behind the classrooms for the eighth and ninth graders. Wonderfully quiet, this was the perfect hiding spot!

One early evening, I dove into the grave concepts of flotation and relative density. Although sinking in confusion, I was determined to swim through, if only I could find a log of comprehension to keep me afloat. I looked up with furrowed brows for divine intervention and froze. Just 15 feet away from me at the end of the cool corridor were half a dozen *langurs*. They had formed a tight circle, making it impossible to see what was happening within. One of them turned around and saw me. I knew just how dangerous they could be, especially at times like now, when they were vulnerable and clearly needed privacy. The only option was to exit the scene by jumping onto the rocks below. Obviously, I couldn't take it. Instead, I became a rock, more precisely, a statue looking down into my books. Did it work? Or did they sense that I, a mere child, was not a threat? I'll never know. But they ignored me. My heart thumped furiously against its cage. Too afraid to breathe, I lived in another bardo, the world between an inhale and an exhale. Strange cries filled the corridor. The gods had intervened once again, giving me the freedom of breathing without ever getting caught. As always, I obeyed. I sighed, then inhaled greedily, the sounds mixing with the cries of the monkeys. Minutes later, they disappeared just as quietly as they had appeared. One looked back at me as if sharing a secret. Was it the same one? Then he leaped off too. A baby clung to one of them. I had just witnessed a *langur* birth!

Dizzy, I walked through the space they had just occupied, which still held their essence like perfume hangs in the air, well after its wearer has passed. I headed down the stairs to the toilets, wanting to throw up. As I pushed the green metal door open, I found a *langur* inside the toilet. He stared back at me, the same stare. Was it the same one? I threw up and ran and ran and ran, WholeHeartWithaHole burning, falling on the rocks, cutting my arm below my elbow, until I reached the safety of the playground.

When I came to, I realized I had merely reached the edge of the playground. Yet it had felt like I had run for miles and hours. How unreal reality really was. How full of lies. How it had nothing to do with how one actually felt. Nothing sensible or logical could explain anything I felt then. Or anything that had happened in my life so far. No wonder, science made no sense at all.

I went back to get my books, the metallic smell of blood still hanging in the air. For my remaining years at the school, I never again visited that spot or those bathrooms.

Midterm results revealed that I had somehow scraped through, managing to pass in physics. But my luck had run out in computer science. The entire class begged the two teachers to give me grace marks, especially asking them to see my diligence and my stellar performance in the Humanities subjects. I was deeply touched. Not only because someone had stood up for me (which was rare in itself), but even more so, because I saw how everyone had come together as a sisterhood to stand up for each other, irrespective of whether we were besties or not. This was the same humanity the *langurs* had shown for each other. It was the first time I understood the meaning of the word 'family'. It didn't really matter that the teachers didn't budge. It didn't matter that from the following year, my marks would be considered to be passing marks, making grace marks and begging for them unnecessary. I had learned the meaning of solidarity.

Worried by my dipping grades, Pup-Pa showed up that Diwali break to tutor me. I understood what a huge deal this was, how many sacrifices Comrade Pup-Pa had made to do this. Both of us worked very hard, doing our best. But I just couldn't understand some of the concepts. Losing his patience, my father hit me. Once. Then again.

I didn't need the purple-blue bruises to tell me how wrong he was. But seeing the broken, fat man collapsing under his many burdens, I couldn't paint him as a complete villain either. Was this because the Tentacle had turned me into a Watcher, a receptacle of all probabilities and paradoxes? Or was it simply a child protecting her parent, her god, to preserve her own reality? Will such invisible responsibilities that children shoulder ever be seen?

Pup-Pa apologized, ashamed. We had dinner in silence with ice cream and a movie. It was his way of making amends. A cycle that would continue until I turned into an adult, concluding with meals in fancy restaurants and five-star hotels in Daman and Calcutta. And in Bombay, in a restaurant overlooking a giant boot in the city's famed Hanging Gardens.

Important Lesson No. 20: ... *life was made up of eatings and beatings, and that the beatings largely predominated.* So concluded Nilkanta, the character in Tagore's (who I learned was a god of a different kind) short story, 'The Castaway'. This was the only ImportantLesson I learned that year from a textbook.

David and Goliath, our rambunctious school dogs and the only monsters scary enough to frighten away the *langur* gangs on campus, showed solidarity in their own way. The furry, black father-son duo fell in love with a skinny brown stray — an ordinary mongrel common to every street in the country, her ordinariness making her blend instantly into whichever landscape she found herself in.

Yet, much to the collective shock of the nuns, didis, spinster matrons and us (the only time we were bound together by something), daddy and sonny had eyes for her and only her. David and Goliath thus taught me Important Lesson No. 21: Love was not being extraordinary, but to see the ordinary as extraordinary.

Many moonlit nights saw the campus awash with the howls of David and Goliath as their two hearts pined for their one love. Finally, the nuns gave in, fixed the bitch, and giving her the name 'Laila', let her into the campus, where the three lived together happily ever after until the ends of their lives.

Winter dawned upon us reminding us that yet another year was ending. Soon, before the water in the pipes got steady, we'd be back home. Such metrics were far more reliable than merely turning pages of the calendar. By now we were wrapping woollen shawls like sarongs over our divided skirt uniforms and sucking in all the mountain sun we could to warm our chilled bones. One way of doing this was to study in the big open playground instead of in the cold Study Hall. I had so many animal memories here. On one side was the house of the toad who had once adopted me but had since moved on to other realms. On the other side was the area where I had witnessed the *langur* birth. On the right side were the steps I had returned to after fleeing a panther attack. Far beyond lay the graveyard. And just before it, a tall wall that mongoose loved to climb at dusk, disappearing into secret homes in thin air after a field day of killing snakes. Was the fauna of the region trying to tell me something? I couldn't understand their message. Not yet.

I set up my stuff by the mongoose wall. After an hour, I finished the last part of my biology homework, painfully drawing the intricacies of the human ear canal and the human brain. Satisfied with my handiwork, I decided to take a bathroom break. Still terrified from the episode of having seen a *langur* in one of the playground toilets, I couldn't use those, even though they were the nearest. I ran to the ones at the far end of the school near the study hall. When I returned, I found my study area isolated, the rest of the girls having huddled far off. I went up to join them. Together, we watched a pair of monkeys curiously open my geometry box, play with the protractor and divider, then drag a compass across the open pages, tattooing their own artistic touches to my painfully executed homework. Helplessly, I watched the monkeys then eat up my homework. One of them turned his head and stared straight into my eyes. We knew we were not to look into their eyes, or ever show our teeth (even in a fond smile) to them. But I could not gaze away until they left.

Luckily, the teacher believed my story. Sure, I had plenty of witnesses, but I didn't have to use them. It was one of the perks of being a teacher's pet! (Except of course, the computer science teachers.)

Sister Bertha, a prickly creature, was like a contaminated needle, who regularly infected our food and needlework — the two departments that she looked after — with her weirdness. Her InPlainSight secret?

She didn't want to be a nun. She'd catch victims in the dungeon called the Needlework Room, pinch the NoMan'sLand by their armpits, just underneath the tricep, and whisper in their ears, 'I am Bertha. Bertha Patel. I was such a rich girl.' And then, leave the rest unsaid; the silence screamed it into our ears '... I don't want to be a nun. Jesus, get me out of here!'

Sister Bertha's little army of cooks combined miseries (theirs and hers) into pots, becoming insanely skilled at awful cooking and doing so consistently. The nuns had a separate kitchen, painted in pretty pink, with fans to fan away a few of the cooks' immediate miseries. Smiling, the cooks poured in this instant relief into the pots and wonderful aromas wafted out of this happier kitchen. Trained by earlier years of eating this food, I had brought with me this year some invaluable life insurance — a small stash of plastic bags, compressed to be even smaller, hidden away from prying eyes under my mattress. Every afternoon, I'd smuggle in a couple in my pocket or under my sweater or pinafore. (The body, after all, as the Tentacle had taught me, was the best place to hide secrets InPlainSight. Nobody saw or heard anything no matter how much the body screamed.) Every day, I'd stash away the most unappetizing *subzi* on my plate into these plastic bags, hide the package in my abundant uniform and ferry them in secret to the pigs. When even the pigs (a species renowned for being less picky eaters than my species) rejected my offerings, snorting rudely and walking away promptly, I jumped in triumph. For once, reality was clear. I wasn't hallucinating and the foods were indeed as unbearable as their boss.

Eventually, the Big Girls couldn't take it anymore. Fuelled more by the awfulness of the food than the food itself, they found the necessary nutrients to create history. One Sunday afternoon, they staged a spontaneous disorganized strike, simply refusing to retire up to their dorms and staying assembled in the square with the Big Girls' Big Bell, saying 'We won't go until we get better food.' Sister Seleena and company came out immediately for this fresh, bizarre piece of entertainment. Immediately, she gathered all the Catholic girls and commanded them sternly to move up to their dorms. They did, like lambs. Sister Superior told me, 'Reetoo, go up!' I was about to, like a lamb, when the biggest of the Big Girls said, 'Rittuparna stay!' I was shocked but more thrilled (and not so secretly either). She was aware of my existence! Not only aware, she even knew my name!

'Reetoo, go up! Now!'

'No, Rittuparna. You stay. Here!'

'Reetoo, I said go up.'

'You stay here, Rittuparna.'

In this power play of egos, I was a mere tennis ball looking helplessly from player to player for ownership, security. The crowd cheered, echoing the biggest of the Big Girls. 'Stay, Rittu,' The very first time anybody had asked me thus, while unknowingly pushing me into a swimming pool of confusion. The deep end of a swimming pool of confusion. A swimming pool outside which grew a tree with SumoWrestlerPalm leaves.

Love and abuse were muddled up into an awful cocktail of sour juice. In my regular, day-to-day life, I couldn't tell the two apart. And so I did not know how to process people or events. What was safe? What wasn't? Who was safe? Who wasn't? What was love? What wasn't? What was abuse? What wasn't? Who was loving? Who wasn't? What was truth? What wasn't?

I did not know who I was, leave alone where I belonged.

My eyes, heavy with apology, guilt, shame and powerlessness, locked in with Sister Superior's before my feet retreated back into the crowd. And what if I hadn't? What if I had listened to my benefactor and not stayed back like a lamb? It didn't matter that the strike was broken up within hours. (No one was punished. Perhaps fans were put in, perhaps fear, perhaps warnings. But the food improved to tolerable levels. The pigs agreed too.) It didn't matter that the matter was forgotten. Had I gone upstairs, that matter would not have been forgotten. Forever, I'd be treated as a traitor, been friendless, shunned, which was worse than being invisible. This is how mob mentality works. Because the worst feeling is that of being rejected and ostracized by a social group — it's better to join the mob and live.

Another experiment occurred that year. Higher powers divided our three-month winter break into two generous halves in December and June, when most schools across India were shut. The winter break was boring and peaceful. I was on cloud nine!

On one of the last afternoons of the school year, I went to grab my nightie — my prettiest one yet, white with dainty blue stars that my grown-up self would think hailed from a Neruda poem — from the peg, to change into for the siesta break, when a lizard leaped off disappearing somewhere. I sighed in relief and changed. Later, when the girls saw me, they shrieked hysterically, almost as if they had seen Shahrukh Khan. One of them grabbed a tall stick from somewhere and shook off something from my left shoulder. A spontaneous concert of shrieks made my feet dance, pushing me to my right. A translucent baby lizard with beady snot-coloured eyes (P's eyes!), the mystery to my short-lived stardom, bravely bounced off at the speed of light into invisibility. I did not know then that this gecko, which had dared to break all boundaries and entered something as private as a nightie, was a time traveller, a warning from the future.

My favourite nightwear lost its beauty instantly. Soon after, I smuggled it carefully into a polythene hidden in a shawl and tossed it into the graveyard next to the Sick Room. Assuming that the *dhobi* had lost it, the authorities let me use my other less extraordinary nightwear. For once, petty matters didn't really concern them because school would be over soon anyway.

Everyone seemed to bounce in delight. A two-in-one delight — the regular joy of vacation plus the new joy of relishing summer holidays with other siblings and cousins for the very first time! Pup-Pa maintained his own record of punctuality, arriving late as usual. Who cared! We were to spend the summer in Calcutta! Calcutta! The city that translated into safety, Big Mother, love and cousins. The Ancestral House, the only sacred space where love and abuse were still — separate. The place where Big Mother's cotton sarees, starched every afternoon on the verandah with the water of freshly cooked rice, dripped a secret into my left ear. That even in stiff, rough places (such as its starchy self) could simultaneously exist (such as its fluffy cotton self) softness and unconditional love.

13

Happy Birthday

As always, the big Ancestral House smelled of rice and deep-fried *rui maach,* mustard oil and very chatty fresh laundry dripping on clothes lines. Ancestral House had half a dozen back-scratching devices, devices I hadn't ever seen (and would never again see) anywhere else! What other secrets did it hold? MultipleSources, as numerous as smells, informed me about what a *phantastic* GetTwoTogether this was going to be because everyone who lived far away (like me and the devils and P) was coming.

Soon enough, they arrived. P looked at me with sheer unadulterated joy and pure love in his snot-coloured eyes. The same snot-coloured eyes as the gecko on the patch of wall directly above his head. Was I the only one putting on a performance? That nothing had ever happened? If you couldn't prove that things had happened, could they have ever happened? *Really happened?* That it had taken me four years to understand that I had been raped? That I had spent the next few months living in a horror film in my mind in which I, a naive child, was convinced that I was pregnant and would need an abortion? That the next few years revealed that I was the luckiest girl in the world to have been spared that shame because I had not yet reached puberty? That I was still a child, unaware of fertility issues and one didn't get pregnant like that. Is there a shop where one can buy words, a sentence as crisp as a freshly starched saree, to convey all of this?

UndiagnosedAutisticUncle bought me a cake from a local sweet shop. A snow-white cake hopelessly trying to be an elegant gateau. A snow-white cake the lusty summer threatened to consume before us. There were no lit up candle tears yet to compete with mine, or the cake's own creamy ones. So really, there should have been no rush to cut it.

Yet I was summoned again and again, each time with the decreasing gentleness and increasing impatience of the immortal pet parakeet, to head upstairs to cut it. Neither of Pup-Pa's brothers were talking to each other. My *jethus* lived separately on each floor now. Once, the hallmark of the Ancestral House had been the joyful hustle and bustle which flowed like an invisible river through its walls, doors and floors and most of all through its warm gaggle of women. Now, its signatures were stony silences and the feelings of a country cut into two.

I didn't know which was weirder. That I preferred to be downstairs with an unbearably cute baby sister, a stranger urinating in my lap—born out of and chaperoned by a mother, her first, my second, who had evolved into the coldness of duty. Or that I was supposed to go upstairs where P, my abuser, was waiting lovingly with UndiagnosedAutisticUncle for me to cut the cake, marking the last year before I entered my teens. The baby licked my face and painted the sleeve of my eggshell Lucknowi *chikan* kurta with spit-up that was almost the same colour as the cake upstairs. I knew the answer. But it didn't matter. Even when you're in its last bits, childhood remains an incarceration.

Humidity made it impossible to breathe or to stay solid. The first day of my extremely heavy periods was bloating me up into a balloon of pain. One tiny prick and I'd burst. A myriad battles were being fought simultaneously, all InPlainSight, yet invisible to the stagnant pond of grown-ups.

Towards the last leg of the siesta hours, one of the *jethus* held his chest dramatically, screaming in painful whispers. Barring the classic insomniacs — the geckos who saw everything, the immortal pet parakeet I couldn't stand and my bookworm self — the whole house was asleep. I dragged myself even as the menstrual heaviness pulled me down with full force.

'Aami gelam. Aami gelam!' (I'm a goner! I'm a goner!)

'*Tumi theek aacho*!' (You're okay!) I said, trying to be the grown-up and not panic. I managed to assist him to sit down on the bed as he gasped and clutched at his chest. He whispered in pain, *'Oshud! Aamar...niye aa. Bachbo na. Chollam. Niye aa!'* (Meds! My medicines, get them. I won't live. I'm a goner. Get my meds.)

'Kothaye?' (Where?)

His hand struggled inside the pocket of his cotton kurta, placed something in my hand before returning to camp on his chest.

'Ne. Niye aye. Tatai tike. Taratari. Ami gelam. Durga Durga.' (Take this. Get it. From Tatai. Fast! I'm a goner. Goddess Durga!)

The local chemist *er dokan* — what they called medical shops there — wasn't far at all on a normal day. That afternoon though, I had to summon up all the strength I could, walking as fast as one could with a boulder the size of a partitioned country dragging them from their ribs downwards. The shop was closed. (It was siesta hours.) So I hopped to the back where he lived and pushed on the rusty round knocker on the dilapidated green door as loudly as I could. Tatai the chemist had nothing to do with chemistry, but like every person selling medicines all over the country, he was called a chemist. What grand title could I give myself then? Tentaclist? (A decade later, I'd land in a country that called people like Tatai pharmacists and their shops, pharmacies.)

The chemist's wife opened the door, yawning. I apologized for waking her up and explained that I'd done so only because there was an emergency. 'Please call Tatai *da* fast. *Jethu more jaabe. Please taratari!*' (My uncle will die. Please hurry up!) A moment later, Tatai *da* appeared at the same spot his wife had just occupied, yawning just like she had. I shoved the prescription into his hands urgently. Rubbing his eyes, he put on his thick-rimmed glasses and broke into a smile. Was he responding to a sweet dream he was in the middle of? What could I do to wake him up? '*Dhut! Boka mein. Eta to Gash er oshud*,' he chuckled. '*Tor Jethur Gash hoyeche*. Hahahaha. *Chinta korish na. Uni beche jaaben*,' he grinned. ('Silly girl, this is gas! Your uncle has gas! Hahahaha. Don't worry. He'll live.')

I walked back with the medication, fuming, wondering whom the joke was on, and who the patient really was. I handed my uncle his meds and retired to the other room without a word. The afternoon played in a loop in my head.

'Jaa!' Pup-Pa said sternly, annoyed at my lack of basic manners and gratitude as the younger devil pulled me by my hand, gently upstairs. 'Come, it's your birthday!' he said lovingly.

'Jaa!' said Pup-Pa.

True to the grown-ups' prediction, we'd outgrown the equations of bullying as silently, as naturally as it had begun. (They had laughed it away then as the petty and cute naughtiness of childhood, unaware that even if the victim and the abusers turn into angels and become BFFs, the abuse itself remains tattooed.) I obeyed Pup-Pa, letting Devil No. 2 help me up the same cold stairs I had once dragged Kaalu up on with so much love and concern. He thought that a solitary bad day had turned me into a spoilsport, unaware that it was a string of bad days turned into a string of bad years. Each familiar step gave me hope. Perhaps I'd be safe now. We're all grown up. So many people are around. (In that ocean of performances, what was one more?) I took deep breaths, the sound of the Bay of Bengal washing over me with each exhale.

'There's our birthday girl!' P welcomed me with much fuss, putting an arm around my shoulder, genuine affection in his snot-coloured eyes, as he laughed through yellow teeth. Where was UndiagnosedAutisticUncle? Where was everybody else? It might have been a trap except that I knew it wasn't. It was late at night, almost midnight, causing everyone to retire after a long day of responsibilities. My legs became iron pillars holding the floors of the broken house together.

'Come now!' I was pushed into cutting my cake, which, like me, was pretending to be so much more than it was. Claps. Noise. My good girl hands moved in obligation of their own accord, feeding cake to those around. Something sweet was pushed into my mouth. I felt weightless. The walls were waves. The floor rose up in joy to hug me, its mosaic in kaleidoscopic glory. A rod grabbed my waist, forcing me up against my will to return weakly to life. Slimy Tentacle tongue thrust into my throat while nightmarish hands grabbed my chest with all the force they could, happy to discover the budding breasts there. They screamed in pain, pouring out saltwater from my eyes. A repulsive fear returned with the familiarity of home. I could barely stand, leave alone scream. My eyes opened weakly and saw Devil No. 2 looking, looking in shock, looking with a poker face, looking away.

When the predator had had his fill, I managed to somehow fight against the insane heaviness carrying all of the weight of gravity, as I feebly climbed down the stairs, holding the walls for support. It wasn't just that I'd been violated. It was as if everything had been taken out of me. Unable to bear this, my body burst from wherever it could. The fire in my heart poured out of my ears. Hot candle tears poured out of my eyes. A bile of helpless fury lay as a pool of vomit at the bottom of the stairs. I held the opposite wall, yelling, kicking and screaming — sounds that nobody could hear. My eggshell *salwar kameez* was now scarlet like an organza party frock had been one Christmas Eve not so long ago.

Ancestral House, the one pristine place I had felt safe and loved in, was now defiled.

I returned to Bombay. Unable to bear a storm without the promise of a rainbow, I undertook my most serious venture yet. In a house that was both ancient and brand new — a two-in-one house. Ancient because it was yet another cool, dark government house with high ceilings and long ceiling fans that the British had built to last longer than they did. New because we had just moved into it, into a new city, into a new locality — at Grant Road in South Bombay. Left for most of the day alone in this NewOldHouse, away from the surveillance of *kakas*, I decided to unfasten the Tentacle's grip once and for all. How? The answer was as always InPlainSight. In a container of Baygon Spray. If a few sprays could murder a family of roaches, surely the tin could murder a toxic tentacle? Definitely. One hundred per cent. I downed it like water. (Two years later, I'd similarly down vinegar with similar results.) Before it could go all the way down, the Tentacle used all its might and pushed it out, making me a fountain of Baygon Spray. The insecticide set my body, Tentacle, WholeHeartWithaHole, all my bits on fire. I downed water — bottles and bottles of it, throwing it all out like an ugly fountain badly in need of repair. The sheer agony! I was dying. Definitely. Hundred per cent. But my body chose its poison, spitting out this insecticide, choosing tentacle poison instead, the 100 per cent guaranteed killer of childhood, over insect poison.

Every cell in my body revolted to this extreme torture, screaming for life. Who knew suicide attempts could make one feel so alive? One hundred per cent alive?

That year, Letitia passed. Everyone was happy for her, though nobody knew how this miracle happened. The answer was, as always, InPlainSight. Her baby sister had finally climbed up the grades to reach sixth standard. It was as if Letitia had been waiting for her all along. With her love and support, Letitia passed and never failed again. The sisters were together in every grade after that.

They tell you that you need to be strong and fight to persevere. But what it takes to survive a storm is the very opposite. To not fight it. This gentleness is the greatest strength there is. To have someone holding your hand through the storm, well, that is love. Only those who didn't have it were acutely aware of it.

14

La La Land

As an expert prey, I knew very well that the powerful are the happiest. By the time I entered La La Land in school at least, some of the power of growing up had begun to trickle in. The biggest, the most mysterious and the most aspirational of all the Big Girl dorms also turned out to be the most beautiful. Everything was painted in custard yellow and light pink, exuding baby love. There was so much light, so much space and a mysterious coolness to the dorm. The thrill of arriving at the finishing line made us giddy.

1. We could access our coloured clothes (for Sundays and special occasions) from special shelves at any time.
2. We could hang out on the cool granite parapets just above the shelves, if we didn't want to nap, and look outside the huge windows.
3. We had our pretty bathrooms painted in matching colours. Our queues for the facilities were shorter.
4. We were allowed to use stuff like Walkmans, read *Stardust*, Mills 'n' Boons, Danielle Steels and Sidney Sheldons. These were still frowned upon, but at least they were no longer *illegal.*

5. Like the Big Girls before us, we also grew to accommodate darknesses with maternal love. The girls rubbed Iodex on my limbs (still aching from Pup-Pa's beatings), rejuvenating them with their love.
6. The didis began to treat us more like comrades.

Meana Didi often showed up blushing and giggling, urging us to ask her why she was so happy. 'Why are you so happy?' we chorused, pressing the magic button. '*Un se milne gayee thi!*' she'd burst out instantly, staring at the floor with exaggerated shyness. In the innocent '90s of small-town India, Meana Didi was bringing alive American concepts of dating which we had only read about in Nancy Drews and Archie comics. I watched fascinated at how this manifestation of meanness had transformed. Clearly, the two weren't exclusive. A person could be both good and evil. Like P. Seeing me stare at the floor for too long, Smriti Singh crept up to me, whispering softly in my ears. 'Ritu, when you grow up, you will also go on dates.'

Shocked, my stare jumped from Meana Didi to her. With her huge eyes, lashes that stretched till Ahmedabad, complexion the colour of milk served to children in loving homes, Smriti Singh had grown up into a classic Rajput beauty. Even in the dull uniforms we wore, royalty oozed out of her. She was already celebrated for her basketball abilities and folk dances. Irrespective of whether they were singular or plural, the didis called all of Smriti Singh's gifts as well as our talents 'GodGift'. (Years later, I'd hear the inhabitants of north India use GodGift as the only excuse and explanation for random things ranging from rain to ingenuity to charm to political parties and Nobel Prizes. Even years later, I'd live in a building called GodGift Tower.) Noor had blossomed into a topper and a renowned scholar. Her besties were now two other girls, also scholars. Already, a school-famous writer/poet/singer, courtesy of the panther, I now also became known for elocution, drama and general knowledge. Without asking us, puberty stole much of our innocence, replacing it, also without asking, with an increasing self-consciousness of how the world saw us.

The biggest of the Big Girls, those in the ninth and tenth standard, were looked up to in general. But those who stood out for their talents, including GodGift ones like beauty, became celebrities the younger ones aspired to be. Thus, the strange local concept of 'Admiring' was born. Being Admired was the ultimate status symbol. Even becoming an Admirer made you automatically cool. Other girls would tease them, 'I know you *Ad-mire* so and so.' They'd blush, like Meana Didi, savouring the attention and saying, 'Stop it, yaar!' The Admirers would show their admiration through gifts — often precious bars of chocolate — which were handed out once a week to Big Girls after having stood in lines for long. Even though the Admired mostly refused these politely (being big sisters) they understood what a huge deal this was. It was a touching gesture because it was all we had. After many attempts, they would cave in, bringing smiles to the faces of the Admirers.

Nobody could predict who'd admire whom. Had it not been so innocent, it might even have appeared romantic.

The two shared a special, quiet bond in which the Admired often gave life advice, guidance and even tuition to the Admirers, being more like big sisters than romantic interests. In that sisterhood, everyone did that anyway in the upper grades. But there was a silent beauty in that special bond.

Around this time, I had my own Admirer, Leela. Grateful to just be around me, she just wouldn't budge until I accepted the bar of Amul Crunch that she had kept safe like gold jewellery. Though the cover with a picture of snowy Himalayas was beautiful enough, Leela had given the bar its own 'case' — a wet handkerchief to keep it from melting — a life hack that I, the Admired, had taught her. Neither of us knew then that Leela would continue to write to me for years after leaving school, until our worlds became so different and engaging that we outgrew the boarding school versions of each other we had in our heads.

Puberty is never a private affair in India, let alone in a conservative boarding school. La La Land's dictator, Sister Eleanor, inspected us more carefully than we watched our own reflections in the mirror while getting dressed. Our nubile bodies were her private business, which she measured with a bizarre set of metrics. God forbid if our uniforms grew even an inch shorter or worse, more flattering! 'Don't show your potatoes to your sirs,' she'd command. She forbade us from lifting our arms in front of the few men on campus. 'Don't tempt your sirs with your potatoes.'

It took me weeks to understand that the potatoes were actually our tiny breasts!

'You! Bring your curves to me now!' Somebody tapped my shoulder, translating her cryptic command. She was speaking to me! That's when I noticed that the loose, ugly uniform that had been like a bed sheet for two years, was finally fitting me like a smart uniform should. Sister Eleanor was more efficient than insurance. Nothing could escape her razor-sharp eyes, especially the things she disapproved of. I had to miss most of morning study time as new, more 'well-fitting' uniforms were found and this one was mended.

I continued going to school in a bed sheet.

During the one-hour siesta, some slept, some rested, some read, and some finished chores (like washing undergarments and writing letters and poems). Most matrons retired to their curtained abodes for relaxation, prayer and other mysterious reasons. Not Sister Eleanor. She would march between the beds, her eyes squinting, her ears perked, all of her GodGift senses on high alert. She caught Rashi holding her neighbour's hand, whose sorrow was obvious to all eyes (except Sister Eleanor's) which could see this was purely a friend consoling another on a bad day. She broke them up immediately with great fuss, had their beds moved away as far away as possible, to the opposite corners of the huge dormitory, and watched them like a hawk for the rest of the year.

With the best of intentions, the nuns led by Sister Eleanor, oblivious to themselves, painted our lives with their collective anxiety about our puberty. We didn't realize that we were being practically raised as nuns. This is why we found romance novels exceptionally fascinating, even aspirational, and discussed them as avidly as the agenda of an underground activist group. Like gossip-hungry colony aunties who can sniff scandal and even manifest it where there isn't any, we caught whiffs of romance, good and evil, where there wasn't any. Consider this…

1. When the handsome Brother of the neighbouring Boys' School brought flowers from their garden and gave it to our most outgoing young Sister, probably for the chapel, rumours spread like wildfire that he had brought red roses for *her*. Within minutes, there was talk of her smiling cheeks matching the colour of the flowers.
2. The sweeper and a didi were exchanging *those* glances. Within a week, it was confirmed that they *most likely* and *most certainly* were dating off campus. Within hours it was confirmed that they were holding hands at places where the nuns couldn't spot them.
3. During the Boys' School Fete when any boy from the (way saner because way more liberal) boys' school offered a hand to a girl to climb up the ledge to the music station, to mention a dedication or a song or make an announcement, it meant he *fancied* that girl. If she responded, they were, most certainly, *in love*.
4. When children from another branch of our school (a co-ed one!) visited ours for an excursion (a girls' boarding school!), both parties visited as if we were on a trip to the zoo. A few of the boys found their picks and wrote letters to them. Friendship between two exotic animal species was unthinkable.

Consequently, perfumed love letters on romantic paper were concealed inside plain, pre-stamped envelopes. Whenever a letter arrived from this address, the person it was addressed to was the last to receive it. With giggles, the letter was snatched from hand to hand, passing like electricity through the collectives of La La Land, as if the letter was for each one of its residents, a love letter bursting with flattery, perhaps even a love poem. By the time it had reached the girl it was meant for, it was dull, crumpled, torn, squeezed dry of any emotion, including romance, that the writer had originally put there.

Some of us escaped La La Land on Sunday afternoons, into the Real World Outside for Social Service. Words have secret meanings, which shift from person to person, dying, being reborn into new meanings their hosts put into them. Service had the same effect on the nuns that special treats like chocolate and ice cream had on us. Outside the school's back gate, beyond the graveyard, lay another dimension, peopled with children from a different world — tribal children. We struggled to teach them the ABC's but they'd rather discuss movies. So I discussed *Beta,* the movie us leftovers had done a PhD on, emphasizing that *Beta* began with a B and its hairy 'hero' Anil Kapoor's name began with A. Thus I stumbled upon a way to bridge the alphabet with movies. They learned A is for Amitabh or Anil Kapoor or *AgneePath*, B is for Bachchan or *Beta* or *Baazigar*, etcetera. It worked like magic on my batch only because children were teaching children.

Oblivious to themselves, children meet other children at their own level all the time. It is growing up which makes them forget this.

On our weekend walk one evening, the nuns took us on the same route to see a special treat. In a small wooden cage, sat a cuddly baby cat, its wildness evident less in its leopard print and more in its fury of trying to tear apart its jail bars in vain, like a heart pumping furiously against ribs, confident that its vigour would definitely break the cage and set it free.

'It's a puma!'

'A cheetah!'

'A jaguar!'

'A leopard!'

'Awww how cute, but!'

'Here kitty, kitty!'

Sure, it was cute, but it was more heartbreaking. How could nobody see the cub's wrath when it was so out there? InPlainSight! My peers were morphing into grown-ups, unable to hold the presence of polarities like children could. Seeing just what they wanted to, ignoring the obvious. I felt just like the puma/cheetah/jaguar/leopard, my pain so bloody obvious, yet rejected, invisible to all around.

We finally got a wonderful English teacher! She imbibed in us a love of Shakespeare, magically making us know *The Merchant of Venice* by heart! Sister Seleena was an answer to one of my many prayers that I wasn't even aware of.

Tall, graceful and reserved, she had the face of a mother duck and a very special tummy — the left side jiggled on special occasions, informing the spectator that in spite of her (almost) poker face, she was genuinely laughing. Apart from Shakespeare, Sister Seleena taught me to look into more than the eyes for clues. I adored her!

One evening, the Normal went to play basketball. The Abnormal sat in a corner, openly exploiting their celebrity status to skip sport. Some girls chatted with a pair of nuns who were around during the few hours when both the rulers and the ruled were carefree together. Suddenly, I heard my name. My ears perked up. Backs were praising me behind my back to Sister Seleena's face. I missed the context but my favourite teacher's response revealed everything. 'Rituparna is only a voracious reader. The really good writer is Gloria, our best so far... way better than a reader masquerading as a writer.' Her tummy jiggled.

Gloria was a pleasant girl who, instead of yelling in disgust had been kind to me when I, her neighbour in the study hall, had vomited in the middle of a smile, just 4.5 inches away from her. I was writing a dutiful reply (a Normal letter from a Normal niece) to P's family. Oblivious to the drama and by GodGift talent, Gloria had shattered my false identity as a teacher's pet. The only teacher I had ever wanted to be a pet to.

Had Sister Seleena seen me hunched within earshot, drowned in a book as always (the only Big Girl in a Green House uniform) and, therefore, done so on purpose? Because she was a cat and my mongrel-like devotion to her made her sick? Or was she simply saying what she genuinely felt, while lying on the answer papers where teachers wrote our futures with their hard, red pens? Somewhere in this mystery, she imparted the last bit of education I'd actually use in my life.

Important Lesson No. 22: Never have role models. Never place a human on a pedestal.

Thus, armed with the most useful part of my decade there, I walked out of La La Land, out of the elegant arched gate of my boarding school where I had once stood in awe, out of the slopes where I was once a runaway, out into the hills to step out into the Real World Outside.

PART III

BOMBAY

15

The Obsidian Fish Bowl

Returning to NewOldHouse, where a school vacation and a suicide attempt had once united in holy matrimony, to make new beginnings was not easy. A rhyme ran in my head. An annoying jingle of an unwanted product. A parting gift from Boarding. A bubble in a polluted river. A nameless present whose name would emerge decades later. Body Shaming/Body Consciousness. Two friends coined a rhyme to honour my legs, which deviated from the syllabus set and taught by film magazines and romance novels, the staple diet of La La Land.

Mote Mote Paav
Meow Meow Meow
Mote Mote Paav
Meow Meow Meow

My legs had transformed from perfect to fat (*mote paav)* almost instantly! Princes to frogs. Words have that magic.

Why were jokes always cracked at somebody else's expense? Laughter was therefore a form of emotional abuse, the worst of all abuses. InPlainSight and invisible, a two-in-one, like the Tentacle I lived with. Perhaps this is why some found tragedy more comfortable. Comedy, with its covert cruelty, bypassed us altogether.

In the NewOldHouse, my teenage years arrived, like aftershocks following an earthquake, ultimately sweeping everything in and out of sight in a tsunami of Shame. It became the only constant. Turning into a mini adult, I silently blamed everyone who did not protect me. That's what being a teenager is about. You act all grown up, shoving down your childhood self while it yells for life InPlainSight. This hot suppressed rage bursts through the largest, most visible organ — the skin. These children of wrath are named Acne. Cute pet names are given — Pimples. To rhyme with other cute things — such as Dimples. Acne and Pimple, cartoon villains. Birthed by the imbalances of the world within and the world without.

My teens was about layers upon layers of Shame which turned into layers upon layers of fat. A 100-layered-birthday cake. A cake without candle tears. As my armour grew bigger and bigger (a Complan girl's armour) the defences of those around me grew smaller and smaller. Aunties with suffixes of Ma and even prefixes of girlhood (with names like Pushpa and Lakshmi) or Mummy (Mummy Aunty married to Daddy Uncle. Did their wedding card read Mrs Mummy Aunty weds Mr Daddy Uncle?), were spilling stories they shouldn't have spilled to a teenager housing a Tentacle.

1. P's sister-in-law said how P hadn't spared her children. Daughters of the brother he loved as much as he loved himself.

2. Ma said how P had tried to fall on her while in the backseat of a Maruti. In the car of a company ironically named after the god of celibacy.
3. One union aunty shared with another aunty, in the presence of my glaring eyes, how *usne* (that person) had taken her by surprise from behind when she was 'her' (my) age. Even now (when she's in her 40s), when she sees him, she wants to punch him where the sun never shines.
4. In a bus, fleshy probes (like the Hand) emerged out of nowhere and dug into Mummy Aunty's legs, her behind and what not. Her *sindoor*, *mangal sutra* and saree, all signs that she was already a man's *amaanat* or property and so must be left alone (like a board saying *Trespassers will be prosecuted*) had done nothing to protect her. Protected by their own superpowers of invisibility, the trespassers were never prosecuted. Since then, Mummy Aunty only travelled in the very front part of the bus where probes were rare and could be seen, prosecuted and shamed. To fight Shame with Shame.
5. A very old aunty married to a Freedom Fighter who had been with Gandhi in jail complained how her PT sir had dropped a pen between her breasts. I wanted to ask her if this was S Sir in a past life trying to perform a physics experiment. But my good-girl convent manners held me back. Days later, the Freedom Fighter husband/uncle who loved everybody would lightly place his hand on my bottom (perhaps mistaking it for my shoulders?)

for a group picture (InPlainSight yet invisible to all) and keep his hand there until the cameraman let us go.

6. Mothers of my classmates from Vapi visited me in dreams, whispering that they had protected their daughters from S Sir by injecting in them the dread of men while they were still in their wombs. They said they had to perform the operation in the womb itself to avoid the accidents that their own caregivers and parents had failed to prevent.
7. Another mother shared what her grown-up son told her — that the aunty they loved and who had watched him for years had 'more than touched' him and done so regularly all the while, genuinely loving and taking care of him.
8. Another aunty vaguely warned me about a union uncle who was very meek and pleasant-mannered, and liked by all and who had just been appointed as my LLG (Latest Local Guardian). Months later, at my favourite Irani cafe, where he fed me my favourite *mawa* cake as always, I'd discover that this aunty was dead right! He'd begun to tell me what a blue film was, when I interrupted him quickly with comments on the lack of purple films and a general lack of purple, my favourite colour, in the world. He patiently smiled, then ignoring me, he went on to explain how in certain areas of Fort, blue films ran regularly. Would I do the honour of watching a blue film with him? (A VIP invite. A chief guest at a function.) I looked down with a poker face at the top his wife had given me

and the CDs in my hand, which his son had burnt for me and whose crush on me was so obvious to all. His gentleness gave me the strength to directly say, 'No thank you, uncle!', as if politely refusing a glass of orange squash, like I had done at his house just half an hour ago!

9. Another aunty said I was a Big Girl now and should be very wary of all uncles. 'If they even hug or kiss you, you could have a baby.' Grateful that I had had better sex education (even if by accident) at age 10, grateful that the fear of being pregnant was now over, grateful for No Baby knowledge and the small but true Own Power it brought, I nodded at her and said, 'Thank you!' She beamed at her own usefulness.

   Years before, I had been in her house, playing outside with her boys, and I had returned with a scarlet stain on my long green frock, my second period after a gap of years. Discreetly, she had handed me a newspaper-wrapped present with a sheepish grin, *'Ab Ritu badi ho gayee hain.'* An official welcome into adulthood! A toast with a sanitary napkin.

   Months later, her husband, who had known me since my childhood, would stare at my innocent, just-forming breasts. Sister Eleanor's voice rang in my ears, 'Don't tempt your sirs with your potatoes' and S Sir's face flashed in front of me. I'd run. WholeHeartWithaHole burning, ordering me to stop this very second, wearing layers in the Bombay summer, flattening myself as much as possible and staying out of his sight, grateful for the many lessons the predators had taught me so early in childhood. Insurance for my youth. One hundred per cent.

10. One more aunty had chai with another aunty and revealed her own version of P during her childhood in Satara. And it seemed she knew many of them. Clearly, P was not a person but a disease, a phenomenon, a virus. Perhaps I should replace P's nickname from Deer (which I had given to him based on his skinny frame when I was five) to Corona.

Stories of abuse would rain on me for life. Way before I had discovered that even my feminist role models, Madonna and Lady Gaga, had both been raped. And years later, married friends would reveal how their bodies were like countries colonized by abuse. How they hated it when their caring husbands touched them gently, lovingly in places where abuse had housed itself lifetimes ago in their childhoods, triggering memories of shame, hate and anger, leaving no space for love. Another told me how her sister was a 'bitter bitch' who hated everyone because she had been raped as a teenager and how she couldn't risk vulnerability to hold on to friendships or any kind of relationships. Why was I a magnet for such stories? Was that which was hidden in me, InPlainSight, visible to others? Was I them and them, me?

The collective's wounds poured into my own 100-layered birthday cake of Shame. An iron corset which got tighter and tighter, making breathing impossible. There was no manual for processing this. I got angrier and angrier, living in hate, blaming everyone who should have protected me/us, completely ignoring the fact that I/we had never told them. I hated everyone and everything! Pup-Pa wrote me off as having a classic case of teenage angst, which must be channelled into something constructive — like fuelling a revolution. An *Inquilab Zindabad*.

People didn't have to literally die for you to lose them. Ever so often, people, the versions you knew of them, died. Leaves transforming through the seasons.

Important Lesson No. 23: Losses were the only constant in life, the one thing you could be sure of.

Somewhere between the losses of my peepul and my carefree self, I lost Pup-Pa as well. Irrespective of the situation, he was at best grumpy, at worst furious. Battles got mixed up. The body translated everything as the same trauma. I screamed back tearfully. He said I could leave if I hated it so much here. I told him I'd had enough of his temper and was leaving. Without waiting for a response, I walked out of the door and out on to the streets. A stray dog in a new territory, wondering if it was claimable. Buildings after buildings appeared and disappeared as I window-shopped. Not one watchman stopped me. Most even greeted me as if I were a resident's friend visiting. Was my class that obvious? Would this work? What doors could my existing skills open? I could teach English, reading, writing, grammar, tutor younger ones. But before that could happen, I had to figure out a place to stay and how to generate immediate income for basic survival. The most pragmatic first step was therefore, to work as a maid — I'd have to teach myself the necessary skills impromptu on the job.

Completely immersed thus, in planning my new life, my legs strolled on the unfamiliar streets on their own, while the rest of me remained dazed. I didn't know then that just a few years later, this would turn into a way of life, of making an unfamiliar city home. A wall with glass shards atop it warned me that I had reached the end of the current apartment complex. Turning around, I saw Pup-Pa! He had followed me all the way! Probably leaving whatever he was doing immediately to not lose track of me. The black Timex dial on my wrist revealed it was already afternoon. He had been following me for almost three hours! With what somewhat resembled a small smile and much awkwardness, we realized we had buried the hatchet. We walked back in silence.

That evening, Patil Aunty, the Happy Family neighbour from Latur, a city legendary for its deadly earthquake, took a sudden interest in me. What began as a dinner invitation for delicious *sabudana khichdi* (like the version Manga Kaka used to make), turned into a beautiful friendship with a family that was truly Happy. With two Happy Children. I began to practically live in her house. The Happy Children brought home a stray cat. She rewarded them with newborn kittens. Happy Family 2 living in Happy Family 1's cozy foyer. The Happiest place in the world! Decades later, I'd discover that suspecting my need for tenderness, which only mothers can bring, Pup-Pa had asked Patil Aunty to watch over me. Across her wall stood another identical home to an identical foyer where I had once tried to end my life. But in her house, we celebrated life. Walls are containers, like tiffin boxes. No wonder, the guardians of history, geckos and spiders favour them. If walls could talk, they would probably never stop. Perhaps they do talk. But you have to know how to listen. That's how you become the keepers of history.

We moved to another government house, for the first time, to an apartment. A very modest apartment in the most posh place I had ever lived at — Carter Road, Pali Hill, Bandra — surrounded by film stars. As I watched Bollywood superstars casually pop up at *pani puri* stalls and at local cafes, and supermodels float around like the skinny trees of Nandurbar, I drowned myself in the magnificent depression of Russian literature and in activism for the victims of the Bhopal gas tragedy. Escaping into the sorrows of others is always more empowering — as if by empathizing with and fighting for others, you somehow do justice to all that you can't empathize with or fight for in your own life.

Ma returned, reborn a stranger, with a stranger Little Sister. Overnight, we were a picture-postcard perfect Happy Family, fit for a Bajaj scooter ad. All strangers to each other; but supposed to love each other.

Years later, my American manager would tell my anxious self at my first American job as a children's photographer, 'Fake it till you make it.' And I'd know that's what all of us were doing in that railway flat in Bandra. Three nuclear families faking it in the hope of making it as one Happy Family. Of course, we never did. Pup-Pa, the head of the family in the way the president is the head of India, was Family No.1. Then Mother No. 2 with one *a*, and daughter, cow and calf, were Family No. 2 with the real power. I, mostly invisible InPlainSight, and mostly outside the suffocating house, was Family No. 3, with zero power. Family No. 1 and Family No. 2 fought non-stop — loud fights which entertained the neighbours far more than the cable TV entertainment they paid for. Everybody was right. Everybody was wrong.

For hours, I'd sit by the promenade at Carter Road, dressed for Saudi Arabia instead of the hip suburb I was in, in T-shirts that covered me till my collar bones — while youngsters around me wore miniskirts and hot pants — looking out at the grey waters hidden under a stinky sea of plastic playing an endless game of peek-a-boo with the waves, looking for answers. The air was so thick with water that you could float paper boats in it. Of course, nobody tried such experiments, the ones that really mattered, two-in-one experiments which mixed physics and geography. The air turned us into rivers. But I continued to dress for Saudi Arabia, being the desert I was.

Apart from a few weeks of respite here and there, the city went through its cycles. Six months of steaming. Six months of drowning. As certain as the rise and fall of the tide in the Arabian Sea. While everybody huddled indoors during the merciless rain and floods, I escaped. In the ankle-deep stream of railway station filth floating inches away, Platform No. 4 of Bandra Railway station was a still raft of serenity, a monsoon child which lived there in its raft form for only as long as the season lasted.

Another raft had once carried Maa, Mother No. 1 with two *a*s. Rafts were good. You could rely on rafts, unlike people. Non-living things can support life better than people. I settled on a bench near the Ladies First Class, the safest spot, with the unconditional love of books carefully rainproofed in layers of plastic in my orange waterproof college bag. I always returned late, as late as possible, but early enough to dodge Family No. 2's silent looks that screamed *Slut!*

During exams, I stayed up nights in the confused two-in-one part-balcony, part-sunroom, mostly studying, staring a lot at strange yellow lights twinkling like bright yellow stars through the foliage, balconies and even the ground. Were they Roadside Romeos? Or just the play of innocent lights? Daytime scrutiny of these places revealed nothing. On one such night, a soft flap and rustle, a two-in-one sound such as I'd never heard before came from the back. My head, still well-trained from a brief stint in *kathak* years ago, turned around as far as it could like a wannabe owl. It was in such shock that the rest of me, Tentacle and all, had to follow. Five feet away from me stood the most magnificent creature I had ever seen. A white owl! How was this even possible? In the middle of the city! 'But there are scanty mangroves by the sea, an abundance of rats to feast upon, so why not?' said Voice of Reason. Everything about it was strange. First, the whiteness; sure there were speckles and grey-brown patches, but it was mostly an eerie white. Second, the size. It was oddly huge, almost two feet tall. Then, there were its eyes — far from the cartoonish adorableness I'd seen in pictures. They were calm, dripping with secrets, messages from other worlds modern humans could never translate. I should have been scared, but I wasn't. The owl was oddly comforting. Two pairs of eyes stared at each other, bypassing time. I knew this was one of my life's most beautiful experiences. The owl visited on and off on some nights, I never knew on which nights. There was no pattern. It passed on something which turned my hair curly, my mind calm, my colour different. It took away the need to dress for Saudi Arabia. It returned what a panther had once taken — my ability to eat animals. Everybody noticed the effects. Nobody noticed the god that had caused them. Except for toddler stepsister whose bladder once woke her up and turned her into a witness.

Love trickled in strange ways. In spite of endless fights with Ma always taking Little Sister's side, her cards of 'Didi and me' were discovered in my textbooks in the middle of class, making my magical new friends (who'd last a lifetime) go 'awww' with such cuteness and me melt in embarrassment. Sometimes Ma wanted to make up and bought us McDonald's burgers. Even then, her partial love revealed itself with everyone's favourite McChicken burgers reserved for her daughter and the cheapest, unloved Chicken McGrill reserved for the loved-for-duty stepdaughter. Love shrunk back.

The owl stopped visiting, as suddenly as it had begun. Perhaps it had completed its mission and now had other missions to fly to.

One late evening, Little Sister and I were walking back home. We had just bought her a notebook from the neighbourhood StoreOfAllThings. Suddenly she squatted, held her tummy and yelled, '*Didi Haggoo*!' I knelt down to her level, unsure whether she had just gifted me a new name, or if she had spotted poop on the street.

'*Maanu Shona Haggoo Shona*,' she said. She had turned poop into a person, conferred to it a surname, Shona, which meant darling in Bengali, for both herself and her beloved poop and managed to make a rhyme out of it. (Years later, I'd be with another toddler, this time my own, who'd be just as obsessed with poop.)

Important Lesson No. 24: Getting down to one's level often reveals mysteries great and small. (Obviously like with most InPlainSight things, grown-ups never get this.)

Little Sister needed to poop urgently. Right now, when there was no bathroom in sight.

'Control, control,' I said encouragingly.

'No!'

'You can do it!'

'Nooo!'

'We are almost home! Hold it.'

'Noooo!'

'Just five minutes more.'

'Nooooo, didi, I can't,' she yelled desperately. Her facial muscles twitched, her eyes looked up in a trance and blobs of poop rained down her small chubby legs. The notebook was the only tool on hand. It was inaugurated at once! I tore page after page, handing it out to her. She obediently wiped it up her leg, collecting shit in it like a tray. 'We are Hansel and Gretel,' I said. She looked at the tiny trail of *Hagoo Shona* trays and smiled. I'm not sure whether at my joke or out of a child's undisguised delight at strange things, or simply at the relief after pooping. The left side of the road, which ended in a dry drain, now looked like a sunken corridor of hotel rooms with food trays left outside the doors. En route to handing her over to Mother No.1 for cleaning, we walked through Carter Road, searching for solace in its bustle. We looked up together. A parliament of small owls had replaced the stars in the sky above us. I knew, I suppose, like one knows a notebook can be a cleaning tool — I knew my owl wasn't one of them.

The Tentacle returned, a reminder that there was no solution. Clearly, the whole world had messed up the roles of the protector with that of the abuser, for weren't, in almost all cases, the men known to the women? And in one case that I knew of, a woman who knew a boy? If not their caregivers and loved ones, then who were the women and the boy supposed to trust? Why were there various degrees of affection, sometimes even a lot of love between the two parties? Why was everything so warped? Why did romance novels and romance movies leave this fine print out?

I became a magnet for more such stories. Stories leaked in silences and performances. Stories a Watcher collected in pieces. Different stories that were the same. Story threads woven together into a thousand-thread-count story bedsheet.

1. Aunty A came alive only when Uncle A was absent. The perfect couple's public mirth and private silent wars were invisible, yet InPlainSight.
2. Uncle B was stringent, proper, aloof unless he was allowed to penetrate Aunty B, which then turned her into a rock. They took turns at melting and becoming walls. I wanted to ask her if they used a

dice to decide their turns, but my convent manners held me back.

3. Uncle C wanted Aunty C to work. When she finally did, he would fight. She said it was because of the compromises made with childcare, housework, etcetera.
4. Aunty D's droopy shoulders strengthened Uncle D's strong ones by submitting to whatever he said, because what was the point of arguing and depleting one's self? It was smarter to accept defeat before a war had even begun.
5. Aunty E's husband was insecure of her independence and fulfillment which meant she didn't really need him at all.
6. Aunty F's GodGift beauty always caught everyone's eye. The more they said how lucky Uncle F was, the more like an ugly, undeserving frog Uncle G felt, and the deeper his imprisonment became. Fights followed like a loyal dog, for random, disconnected reasons.

A Collection of Emotional Abuse Stories. A Collection of Patriarchy Stories.

They attacked me with their poisoned arrows. (Like the ones in mythology television series that had hypnotized me.) My heart went out to both the uncles and the aunties. Both were suffering, both were victims of patriarchy. If grown-ups were so messed up, then what hope was there in growing up at all?

What was the point of living in such a world? I had had enough, had nothing to look forward to. With the sweetness of boarding school fading off into an old memory, like a book read years ago, I lost all hope. I stepped into college — got on and off local trains, buses and shared taxis and endless streets — a goldfish in an obsidian fish bowl, gorgeous, opaque — the kind that made one wish for the regular bars of a cage through which one could at least see outside — with no room to grow, not knowing where the liquid darkness ended and the solid darkness began.

16

Seppuku

The Tentacle was an evil witch. In the obsidian fish bowl, it made me discover several new words — Kamikazee, Harikiri and my most favourite, *Seppuku*. Beautiful words with stories, techniques and foreign spellings. New words for one first overheard in peepul days: *Sooeeside* (a needle on the side). The old and the new, both set me diving into a sea of research. On an unruled sheet (because I couldn't bear any more rules, not even on a page) I narrowed down my research to make a list of My Favourite Things, different from the lovely one in *The Sound of Music* movie. A list to fly out of the obsidian fish bowl once and for all.

1. Jump off rooftops of tall local beauties: Victoria Memorial, Gateway of India, the Taj Mahal Hotel
   Pros: Foolproof!
   Cons: A serious danger of homicide lurked in this *sooeeside* method. What if one falls upon a passerby or two and unwittingly kills them too?
   Cons: Ugly as hell. To let the living live, one must die with some beauty and grace.
2. Hang myself with a purple pashmina from one of the myriad tall ceiling fans I grew up with (and which brought negligible Relief in summer).

Pros: This would greatly elevate the self-worth of the vintage ceiling fan by finally manifesting its usefulness.

Cons: Hanging, even with a pretty purple pashmina, made the victim appear ghastly.

Also, there was no guarantee that the skeletal fan itself might not commit *sooeeside* instead of the person and fall with them (alive!) onto the ground, causing unwanted fractures.

3. Stick yourself into a *tandoor* or an ordinary oven.

   Pros: This method has stood the test of time, first appearing as a homicide attempt in *Hansel and Gretel*. Then, tried and tested successfully outside of a fairy tale by the poet Sylvia Plath.

   Cons: Ghastly! For the sake of loved ones, it's kind to die in beauty.

4. Gunshot: Get a rifle from an army uncle and shoot yourself in the head or in the mouth.

   It would be an entertaining exit. Plus red, even if a pool of blood, always adds colour to the face.

   Cons: There are enough stories of bullets being lodged in the head and the person living on with migraines, strokes and other unnecessary burdens.

5. Overdosing on sleeping pills.

   Pros: Same as above.

   Cons: Same as above.

6. Potassium Cyanide.

   Pros: Foolproof! Immediate!

   Cons: Horrific sight. For the sake of loved ones, it's kind to die in beauty.

7. Strychnine.
   Cons: Hard to find.
   Nor was its work necessarily immediate. It might take 15-60 minutes to work. And as in 4 and 5, there are serious risks of surviving and living with brain damage, kidney failure and other unwanted atrocities.
8. Carbon Monoxide.
   Pros: A sure shot exit! And perhaps one could simply try a gas pipe!
   Cons: Procurement. Finding a space (tent, closed car) that won't endanger others.
9. Throw yourself in front of: A car on a freeway or a Huge Speeding Express Train.
   Pros: Immediate! Foolproof!
   Cons: Ghastly. What if they mistake your body for somebody else's?
10. Burying myself in a bottomless pit of confetti.
   Cons: Lots of work in first finding and then filling up a pit bottomless enough for so much confetti.
   Pros: Beautiful exit! True to my life's theme of the unseen lying InPlainSight. Therefore, my favourite.

I closed my eyes and returned to Eden, under a pet tree. The only place I'd want to rest. A ghost with GreatestRegrets planning next life without Greatest Regrets.

17

The Wedding

'They're coming! It'll be amazing!' My father's delight drenched me, in spite of my own torment, making me realize I was a sponge, and that I had always been one, absorbing energies around me, letting them overwhelm me.

I stood on the platform with a little army of Western Railway *kakas*, holding a small, perfect wooden beam (meant to create perfect railway sleepers) with a white metal board on which in English and Devanagari scripts, a pair of *kakas* had carefully stencilled in the unique shade of government maroon paint, 'Welcome P, M and family.' Pup-Pa's blind love couldn't see how strange this was. But passengers and passersby did, staring at us in amusement, turning their heads to get their fill for a little longer, even as their legs had moved on. Some of their faces, especially their wandering, wondering eyes, revealed what they were thinking: Film shoot? Where are the cameras? Oh my god, is there Shahrukh? Hrithik? Salman? Another star? Hidden cameras?

Only garlands (normal for senior union comrades like Comrade Pup-Pa) were missing for a complete VIP welcome. I should have been mortified! But the Tentacle protected me with a mini panic attack instead, throbbing in my throat, freeing the dusty grey platform from the clutches of gravity, moving it up to meet my face. I rushed to the tracks to vomit.

Like a favourite mix tape, my mind played out the list of Favourite Things. Playing out your death enough number of times, watching yourself die, can be strangely liberating. It brought me back to life. Death often does that, if you let it. A worried *kaka* asked me if I was okay. 'Okay,' I said. 'Okay,' he said. An OkayRainCloud hung above us, pouring okayness all over the railway platform. Another *kaka* knew tap water was NotOkay for *sa'ab's* daughter, so he brought me Okay water — a bottle of Bisleri. I hoped he had bought it from the allowance Pup-Pa had given him for the almost-VIP event. I gratefully accepted the water with a smile. 'Okay, thank you, *kaka*.'

There were many kinds of kindness. Ironically, the ones who had the least to give had the most compassion. It was almost a law, like Newton's Law of Motion, waiting to be named a Law. Important Lesson No. 25: One side effect of living at the mercy of endless higher powers is unconditional compassion for fellow beings.

'Oh *Maaa*! How beautiful you have become!' M remarked, bouncing off the train to embrace me. 'And your eyes,' she said, looking at them while holding my chin. '*Ki shundoor!*'

'What a beautiful lady she has grown up into!' I heard a snot-eyed voice say. I wore a plastic smile like make-up, grabbed their luggage and neatly side-stepped the hug that the snot-eyed creature threatened to give me. The Tentacle had brought me up well. So well, that back home when P stared at my legs, now returned to freedom in psychedelic cycling shorts and said, 'Not at all!' to Pup-Pa's remark of me putting on weight, my legs walked themselves to my bicycle (ironically named Devil) to ride off in the colony. So well, that even when I was asked to accompany him to Bengali Sweets to buy *mishti*, I suddenly remembered a British Council lecture I simply had to attend all the way in town and, therefore, had to rush to take the fast train on time. Instead, I hung out reading at Platform No. 4 as usual. So well did I manage things that during all of P's entire stay, *nothing* happened because either I was out of the house or I was with everybody else. Never alone with him.

The Tentacle raised me well, merging with the lessons of Sister Eleanor, keeping me safe.

1. Safe enough to never step into a car full of boys I knew. (Two girls would later tell me how they had done the opposite while tipsy and how it had turned out to be a huge mistake. Sometimes, something happened to Perfectly Good Boys, especially in spots by the sea: Carter Road, Bandstand, Worli Sea Face.)
2. Safe enough to never stay out late, unless accompanied by half a dozen girls.
3. Safe enough to only head to Razzberry Rhinoceros during the day or early evenings, that too, only if pressurized horribly (which was rare) and unable to fake period pain, upset stomach, fever, etc. successfully.
4. Safe enough to always walk with a folder shielding my potatoes.

5. Safe enough to always carry enough sanitary napkins to last a period, consequently never having to worry about a garment turning scarlet ever again.
6. Safe enough to become a warrior carefully shopping for weapons. Beautiful, sharp Beak Clips. Potent weapons in disguise, strategic, and easy to hide in hair.
7. Safe enough to become an alligator and attack a faceless stranger (like the Hand) where the sun didn't shine with the Beak Clip, even when he didn't do anything. But that didn't matter because the Tentacle said he would have, just a few seconds later. And like any sensible country I must be prepared to attack before the enemy did.
8. Safe enough to always stay in crowded spaces, in daylight... regular stuff Indian girls were taught at puberty by other girls, but I had grown up simply knowing. Thanks to the Tentacle, my formative years were much safer than those of most girls in India.

The Tentacle also failed me. Unable to protect me from being an Indian girl in India:

1. At railway stations when faceless strangers (like the Hand) were running to get on to their impatient local trains to take them to parks, homes, interviews, offices, funerals, schools, temples or whatever, and found a nanosecond to expertly push against my chest, throwing its shield off, even as they barely managed to jump onto their annoyed trains which,

like waiting-girlfriends-throwing-fits, had already begun to walk away from the platform.

2. One night, the Tentacle did not warn me about avoiding walking the side street to take the back gate into my colony at 10.30 p.m., usually a very crowded and safe hour for the neighbourhood. A pair of Perfectly Good Boys turned into RoadsideRomeos appeared out of nowhere! They were circling in on their prey on a Kinetic Honda, taking rounds all around, calling me Sushila and Nirmala and singing songs foreign to convent girls, trying to touch my potatoes, but managing only to scrape my scapula. I raced to the safety of the back entrance, reaching the sanctuary of my middle-class railway colony. Safe, I breathed finally, a frightened deer who had managed to escape from the clutches of wild dogs.

Months after P and M's eagerly awaited and GodGift departure to their own Perfectly Good Boys, Pup-Pa's delight once again drenched me like a sponge. Only this time, it mixed with my own joy and Family No. 2's. Big Mother's Big Daughter was going to have a Big Wedding, meaning another exciting *phantastic* GetTwoTogether. It is possible to be frightened and relieved, miserable and ecstatic at the same time. Frightened to return to the Ancestral House, my refuge until a birthday spoiled it all. Relieved because history hadn't repeated itself during P's last visit. Miserable because P would be there too, ecstatic because so would everyone else I loved.

Big Daughter was the first daughter of the extended family, the first niece when some like M and Pup-Pa had been teenagers themselves. Everyone, therefore, loved her a little extra. Upon landing in the Ancestral House, I saw that even the walls had swelled in extra happiness than they did for other special celebrations. The flowering trees which, like Big Mother, were too short to be trees or mothers, were overflowing with hibiscus joy. The ancient red floor in the balcony was redder, nourished by the drippings of talkative sarees, which as always had formed little puddles here and there, holding the promise of innumerable secrets that the ravenous sun would eat up, refusing to share. The rose-necked parakeet defied time, remaining ageless and annoying. He screeched at the sight of me, desperate for the treats my ears held. Dangling ceramic red chillies. Convinced that they were the real thing, the chillies taunted him, like ads for flashy new cars selling consumers false promises of happiness.

An incense smoke cloud gave Big Mother a halo which should have lasted forever. Big Mother's love, as certain as sunrise, washed over me and everything around. The Smell of Relief. Ruby-studded gold discs in her ears had made tall slits in her lobes, matching those that Pup-Pa made into chicken breasts to help the marinade soak through and through. Like those spices, these slits threatened to go right through any minute, splitting her lobes into a fork — wiggly Y-shaped ears. Somehow, like me, they held on, not just through the wedding but forever. Defying time like the parakeet that loved them.

They held me transfixed even when we went to Barasat to visit Pup-Pa's brother. A *maatir manush* who lived in a *maatir bari*. A simple man of the land who lived in a house of clay. He turned out to be Pup-Pa's doppelganger in looks and political ambitions, as a sarpanch and Marxist.

Amar bari tomar bari Naxalbari.

Yet (in spite of *kakas* and all) we had never been treated with such royalty (as our ancestors had during their glorious feudal past). Men as skinny and dark as the barks of the trees around, caught fish fresh from a pond painted green with algae and with the reflections of the hundreds of trees all around. The lucky ones were released. The chosen ones were tossed into a *chowacha*, a three-foot tall cement tank, a makeshift aquarium as crowded as a Bombay local where they throbbed like a litter of Tentacles until eaters chose their preferences, transporting prey to the lunch table.

In another *chowacha*, constructed in our Vapi house to hold water during the hottest months as insurance, a lizard had bobbed up and down just like them. I had screamed, recognizing the dinosaur within, screamed and screamed. Vishnu Kaka, scared by my shouts, had come to the rescue, like the god he was named after, and fished it out of its air-conditioned pool. According to rumours from the other *kakas*, Vishnu Kaka had been cured of leprosy, though he looked as fit as a fiddle, and had the uncanny ability to cook cheap fish and make it taste magically like Chicken 65. The same dish which was extremely delicious until S Sir had had it before meeting me at the guava tree.

No amount of cajoling, coddling, pleas, raised eyebrows, faces of disbelief and exhaustion, whispered taunts and loud taunts, could force me to taste a drop of any of the fish curries, leave alone nibble on a Tentacle-lizard-*chowacha*-Chicken65 fish. I stuck to the dal and rice with ghee, delicious Comfort Food, and then, gazing at the countless coconut trees outside the window, expressed a wish for fresh coconut water. Another skeletal man, with the colour and strength of a tree trunk, promptly appeared out of nowhere, climbed up a coconut tree, with way more grace and otherworldly skill than even the arboreal creatures I'd gone to school with, and disappeared into the top of the tree like Homeless Peacock/Water Phoenix. A few breaths later, he reappeared with a green *daab*, produced an iron knife out of nowhere, cut the fruit open and handed me the freshest coconut water in the world. He topped this with a smile, like the moon shining in the night sky.

Turning her lips fuchsia with the thinnest paint brush I'd ever seen, Big Daughter asked me to accompany her to the beauty parlour — my first trip there! New words such as threading, waxing and facials entered my vocabulary. But the most fascinating of all was that it was a marvellous world of women. Totally safe! One hundred per cent. Then she bought me my first heels and gave me a new life. Lifebuoy and Cinthol were finally dethroned.

In becoming a house hosting a wedding, the Ancestral House had returned to the loving refuge it had always been before a certain birthday. All the chatter, the hustle and bustle of a million preparations, laughter, shopping lists, guests... And now me, avoiding going anywhere with P (even if accompanied by a battalion of cousins and aunts). Even while getting treats like jewellery boxes and tables of carved Kashmiri walnut wood and sandalwood, and furniture of carefully picked Burmese teak. One afternoon, just before heading out on one such adventure, P chilled me with a remark, casual to all ears, but mine. 'She dresses nicely there also (psychedelic cycling shorts in Bombay) and here (midnight blue *salwar kameez* with white rosebuds in north Calcutta) also. She dresses as per the occasion, people and place,' he said with a warm smile. With a poker face, a Tentacle throbbing in my throat, tears of fear and rage, I walked back unnoticed. Knowing that even with Own Power and the freedom of being a teenager, I was still under the roving eye of my former predator; therefore, still a prey.

Somebody said I was wanted in the living room. Unknown to me, the Tentacle had turned me into a superb actress. A knower of secrets told by dripping sarees. Acting irritated, dusting the dirt from my eyes, I stepped on the stage: the mosaic-floored living room where emotions, opinions and heated debates decided the beallendall — the Wedding Menu. Each food item auditioned like desperate actors for a role in a blockbuster movie (a wedding movie, a *Hum Aapke Hain Kaun*). The *jethu*-in-charge would shift his entire weight to one side, fart, make the final decision on one item (Main Course: *Kosha mangsho*, Bengali biryani, *chingri malai* curry, fish steamed in banana leaves). Then he'd shift his weight, release wind equally from the other side too, to be fair and make the final decision on another set of items (Appetizers: *Macher chop*, banana flower cutlets, deep-fried aubergines). Back to the first side (Dessert: *rasmalai, roshogolla, mishti doi, nolen gurer, payesh/* ice cream). Repeat until the entire Wedding Menu was ready. '*Uff aami gelam*! I need my medicine,' he wailed. In clear need of Relief, amidst peals of barely stifled, affectionate giggles, he sent me to the same chemist I had visited on a birthday not so long ago to get first aid for his *gash*. This time, I walked leisurely knowing nobody was dying and that I had freed myself from my predator's attack.

I put a curse, a two-in-one curse. A *good* two-in-one curse: P would never attack me again. NeverAgain. Nobody else would attack me either. NeverAgain. No black holes sucked these up (unlike a first *kolera* curse) with a gravity straw. The twin curses floated freely in the Milky Way.

PART IV
FORGIVENESS

18

Grown-uphood

Forty-eight seasons later, I peered out of the Hobbit house window of a Lufthansa whale and said goodbye to the twinkling stars below. To the billions of stories they were powered with. Stories of kind friends and editors I had accumulated as lifelines, under whose tender love and care (TLC), I had bloomed like Letitia. Stories read, written, dreamed up, brooded upon and lived out on Platform No. 4. Stories of the city where flatulence was cared for like a pet and had a pet name, of Ancestral Houses, of many mothers and Big Mothers, of sarees dripping starchy secrets, of birthday cakes with no candle tears and molested birthday girls with candle tears. Stories of the city whose roads my feet had painted with unbearable purple gloom for years, until it loved me and became my first real home. Stories of the cruel city I had fled to, where the alienation of the devils' house returned, of the landladies with happy names (Pinky Chaddha and Simple Chopra) and whose sons with normal names (like Amit and Rohit) stole from her tenants, of Fascist Boss Editors gagging me with duties that weren't mine. Stories of a city, which clipped wings so badly that I had to board a whale to fly away from the country it ruled. Stories of the best friend with kind eyes I had married because he had loved me like Big Mother did, like Pup-Pa should have, like Ma only claimed to have had and who now sat next to me on the cinnamon-smelling whale plane headed to Munich, where a twin sister whale plane waited to carry us to San Francisco.

With the precious thud of immigration stamps on our passports, the St Bernard immigration officer welcomed us into the American Dream. Unknown to me, an invisible Tentacle had entered America as well. On a Tentacle Visa. Defying the 23-kg Lufthansa luggage limit. Defying the sharp sniffer dogs, the world's only unfriendly Labradors. Defying space-time, defying the laws of physics and logic.

And so:

1. New freedoms yearned for so long, fizzled like soda bubbles. The freedom to walk on stunning streets with the luxury of getting lost on them (with zero fears of assault). Streets strewn with fruits and rainbow flowers, lined with trees, covered by teddy bear clouds soaring in a blue sky. Streets staring up at green mountains. All swallowed up suddenly by a giant balloon of gloom, as familiar as family. How could one be so desolate amidst so much perfection? Defying space-time, defying the laws of physics and logic? Cumulus teddy bear clouds turned black with rage, melting into tears of paralysis.
2. GetTwoTogethers after GetTwoTogethers filled with genuine laughter, glamour, two-in-one gourmet home cooking and music obnoxious enough to drown out shadows, screams and truths — where elegant wives (Big Mothers-in-the-making) dripped love

and applause for mundane feats — felt Sisyphean. How could one be so terribly lonely amidst so much camaraderie? Defying space-time, defying the laws of physics and logic? The tears cried in secret in the bathroom burned the rotis in the kitchen.

3. Finally having my own house gave me Cheshire Cat grins. Which soon disappeared in bits like the Cheshire Cat until the joy wasn't there. Keeping the house felt Sisyphean. Gas leak threats, termite attacks and jarring fire alarms took over the beautiful historic homes with lavish lawns.
4. Learning to drive through the generous grey ribbons of suburbia should have been easy, especially after having navigated through so much Tentacle crap. But it was sheer terror with complete breakdowns at every turn. The husband, strengthened by a lifelong diet of power-packed parathas, bore each panic attack like Big Mother, and somehow taught me to drive. Somehow the DMV granted me a licence marked 'Very Good', impressed by my abnormal alertness (a gift from the devils and P). But even decades later, I'd break down, overwhelmed. PTSD manifested in parallel parking, tight spots, allowing it to rule my life, making me opt to stay home.
5. In spite of gorgeous, heated, luxurious, big, semi-private, tempting pools, I couldn't learn to swim.
6. Having the most beautiful baby in the world, who visited me in dreams before he was born, whom I wrote letters to while I still had two beating hearts (one WholeHeartWithaHole, one whole heart), who turned me into an inventor of names (Poubloo,

> Roubloo, Ghouploo, Gibblee Dibblee, Frownie Brownie, Mamaroo. Grumpysaurus, Fussypants, Fluffpot, WMD (Weapon of Mass Distraction), who taught me what love was, proving the cliché that you don't know what love is until you have a child, whom I loved more than anything, who turned me into Big Mother, who was everything dreams are made of and yet, who wasn't enough for a Tentacle. I'd cry for hours holding his tiny fingers, reaching out from the gap under the locked bathroom door in heartbreaking support.

I had moved on, I mean literally to another continent. In the language of Indian grown-ups I had *settled down*, like dust, and even had an *issue*, like a magazine. Yet, the past never left, always living inside me. Like a mad dethroned king in his palace ruins. Like a Tentacle. Does the past ever leave the tomorrow? Perhaps the elders of the elders of the elders... the ultimate elders, the ones who had birthed words and their meanings, knew this. That's why they put the same word to mean both yesterday and tomorrow in both Bengali, *kaalke*, and Hindi, *kal*.

The Tentacle visited at inappropriate hours — when hosting a barbecue, when greeting guests at birthday parties, in the middle of an interview, when the world slept; at times, when I had to put on performances, never saying, 'Inconvenience caused is highly regretted,' to its Railway Kid host like the Indian Railways did to its passengers. Like many, I had heard Silly Con Valley yell, 'There's an app for that!' Only upon *settling* here did I discover its far louder whisper, 'There's a (medicinal) drug for that.' Those with real shrinks taught me that depending on their intensity, my symptoms were those of an anxiety attack or a panic attack. Trembling with palpitations, drained with fatigue, choking with terror, overwhelmed with small responsibilities, I swam in an ocean of worries, the size of the Pacific, about all the things that could go wrong. The Tentacle gave me panic attacks and anxiety attacks without valid reasons. In the middle of what was, supposedly, Paradise. For fears that were nowhere in sight except InPlainSight in my body. I responded to a tiger which wasn't in the room. I became used to these visits like one is to a ghost living in the storeroom of their house — locked, dark, forgotten, but very much there. During those surprise visits, I was living a life on the outside that ticked all boxes of Normal (various shades of settled — settled with marriage, job, house, car, settled in Emerika, settled in Silly Con Valley) while simultaneously dying, strangled by an invisible Tentacle in the secret world inside. An InPlainSight-secret-world made of anxiety bricks cemented by panic.

One fine Californian day, It 2.0 happened. It 2.0, which defied reality and everything I'd ever known. It 2.0, which would change my life forever. I was driving to Stanford, at rush hour, for an interview. Without warning, like an accident, the road turned into an infinite cobweb of white roots, invincible veins of time sticking out of a floor they had rendered invisible. Everything — fellow rush-hour passengers in their metal boxes, buildings, natural trees — transformed into giant glistening trees with skirts of mysteriously glittery fluff in a shade of white I couldn't place. I walked around, dressed in a skirt of the same mysterious glittery fluff in a shade of white I couldn't place, happy as the teddy bear clouds in the Mountain View sky above my car. There were two of me! In two places! At the same time! I looked at Me. Me looked at I. Both felt everything the other did:

1. The foreign coolness of Me's world on glowing translucent skin. The car heater of this reality on I's tanned opaque skin.
2. The foreign smell of mysterious glittery fluff which could most closely (but not accurately or completely) be described as floral scents. The smell of Earl Grey, car smoke and a mélange of morning city smells.
3. The foreign sound which could most closely (but not accurately or completely) be described as the sound of a breeze and silence and the essence of a flowering tree. The white noise medley of morning city sounds — cars driving, buses stopping with loud sighs, a rare honk, the city's raucous gas-powered leaf blowers, the cacophony of construction…
4. The foreign taste which could most closely (but not accurately or completely) be described as the serene crisp coolness of mountain air. The leftover taste of Earl Grey and raspberries.
5. The foreign support of a floor of a cobweb of roots could most closely (but again not accurately or completely) be described as Play-Doh, yet solid. The foreign feel of the trees could be most closely described as the coolness and smoothness of glass but not its weakness, because it was super solid.

> Here, I was supported by the floor of a mundane car floor mat and a grey leather driver's seat.

One was the physical world, the other a magical world which defied all the laws of time and space. It would have been a hallucination had it not been so lucid. I felt and processed every single thing equally in both worlds. How could I be in two places at once?

My phone rings through the R-class's bluetooth speaker, the interviewee's assistant is on the line, voice booming through both worlds, gently demanding where I was. Me watches I look around to realize and say that I have entered Stanford. The assistant gives directions. I drive through the university's lanes and stroll on the floor of the unreal forest, thoroughly lost in the former, completely at home in the latter. How did I know my way around so well in this foreign forest? Where I did not even know the trees. Or the floor. The assistant called again to repeat the directions. Perhaps she was psychic and had sensed this collapse of time and space. I follow her directions, but soon realize that I'm driving around in circles. She calls again. The scene repeats itself a few times until the last call when the meeting is cancelled and rescheduled. I am thoroughly lost but somehow find my way out and back home. All the while I am staring at Me. I call my husband. He listens patiently, sweetly praising my imagination that had stayed intact through the journey into grown-uphood unlike most adults he knew. He reminds me how he's always loved this about me, so much. We hang up like couples who have been married for a while do, ignoring how both have misunderstood the other.

Orbs of light and balls of colours I can't place fill the corners of my eyes. When I turn my head to focus on them fully, they disappear, content to live only in my peripheral vision. Beauties without ambition.

These visions travelled with me, changing all the time. Every now and then, an otherworldly whiteness swallowed everything. Becoming everything. When I closed my eyes. When I opened my eyes. Even when objects could be seen, this whiteness surrounded them. It reminded me of haloes around the head of Jesus Christ in the pictures at my boarding school. Perhaps that's what they were. Haloes. Sometimes these haloes changed into pastel colours like the orbs. Gentle ringing filled my ears, deafening me. I began to hear whispers! Whispers I couldn't comprehend. Behind me were vapour-like presences I couldn't see, couldn't explain but I knew they were there. Ghosts? Terror turned me cold. A panic attack wrung the residents of my chest until the entire neighbourhood screamed in pain. My heart, WholeHeartWithaHole, began to beat with the paranoia of a mad animal.

The walls shook like waves. A Chilean friend who had grown up in Italy floated into my memory. In his childhood, he'd witnessed a massive earthquake during which the walls had danced like waves. I lived in an earthquake zone. Minor tremors were routine, but I'd never seen a big one. Was this a major earthquake? The doors, the glass, the table, everything danced together, each to separate, individual beats somehow tied together into a common rhythm. The floor turned to the infinite cobwebs of white velvety roots. No, this was something else altogether. In the space between the dance, I saw small dots floating, like wisps of cotton, like confetti atoms, like germs in a microscope, like travelling sperms on TV. Yet they were none of these. Months later, when this would become routine, I would realize that what I had seen was energy. But right now, as everything I knew about reality crumbled, I was utterly petrified! I hadn't been this afraid since my stay with the devils. No, even there, there was solace in solitude. So this was the most scared I'd ever been. Certain that I was going mad, I called my closest friend, nervously explaining my symptoms. She berated me. So did the others — who were less close — I reached out to. Everyone dismissed this as another of my quirks or as hallucinations. Nobody believed that my hallucinations were perfectly lucid. Only the baby didn't judge. His chubby cheeks validated the reality I could barely validate myself. The validation I suddenly realized I had sought my whole life, from others. He gave me full acceptance, staying present with me with all of his dimpled baby fat, in a way adults never could. As I went back to all the times when adults had failed me, I realized that this was all I had ever wanted from them. But even then, I realized they were incapable of this because those adults could barely be there for themselves.

Once again, I felt helpless — as if I were in the devils' home. 'But I am in grown-uphood now,' I reminded myself. What was the one power my adult self had over my child self? The answer surfaced like a bubble in a lake. Information! I dove in right away. My shaky fingers surrendered my symptoms to the grace of Google:

1. Hallucinations.
2. Hearing, seeing, smelling, tasting and feeling things that aren't there.
3. Withdrawal and struggling with the basics of life (old, lifelong symptoms).

Out popped the top explanation, like toast out of the toaster.

'*... a chronic and severe mental disorder that affects how a person thinks, feels and behaves... may seem like they have lost touch with reality... Although not as common as other mental disorders, the symptoms can be very disabling.*'

I had managed to catch one of the first diseases I had learned about. Skizzofreneeah! A side helping of paranoia in quantities I'd never known to exist came in. My hands began to shake again, like those of old people who had lived too long. The loss of my mind seeped into my body with currents swirling all over from my toes to my scalp and beyond. How could I feel what was beyond my body as my body? Sometimes, it felt as if worms as heavy as Sumo wrestlers were crawling all over me. Mostly, it felt like my baby had when he decided to stretch in my womb. I was grateful that I had had the privilege of pregnancy: it helped me process this madness that had come alive in my body. Was I possessed? My feet and hands pulsated with electricity. Matter disappeared. Doors, windows and tables didn't bother with the politeness of performance this time. They didn't dance. They simply vanished.

Then they returned. Then they disappeared again. Only the whiteness was constant. The whiteness I had always imagined mental asylums to have, where shocks turned crazy minds into white canvases. I was going mad! I certainly was!

Somehow, I managed to summon a strength I didn't know existed. Struggling badly, I made it through the duties of the day. Somehow, I managed to fall asleep. Something old and known, yet new and unknown visited me with the familiar silence of smoke. I soared over a gorgeous lush green hillock, parts of which were hidden, playing a sort of peekaboo with the clouds. Here and there, amidst the unbelievable shades of the green of the trees, were hundreds of thousands of papers floating in space with the mist. A little lake with glassy water reflected the clouds, the forest and the pages. Gold shimmered in its middle. A mirage in real water! Something magnificent was rising out of it, something in brilliant glittery colours not of this world. Gold, fuchsia, purple, yellow, blue, green, myriad shades, all at once. Something I couldn't name or place. Something of another world... someone I knew from a long time ago. I could not see myself anywhere. Yet I knew I was there. I was the mist. I was the pages. I was the forest. I was the water mirror. I was nothing. I was everything.

I woke up breathless, unable to handle so much ethereal beauty! The last 24 hours had been one long lucid dream. I could no longer tell the real from the unreal, the dream world from fantasy. Eerie, deafening scratching sounds came from outside the bedroom window, betraying the serene blood moon which shone through the swaying trees into the room, leaving a pool of moonlight on the floor for scattered toddler toys to play in. Following the cues of my inner child, who had been hypnotized on such nights by a tree, I too, walked to the generous bow windows, spellbound. The small copse of skinny trees swayed merrily like tipsy aunties dancing at a party. Below me, separated by a mere wall, were two huge raccoons engaged in a bloody fight, using the wall as a shield. I screamed. My husband woke up, unfazed. A paratha-powered man with Punjabi confidence, who always knew just what to do. He grabbed the water bottle beside him and bathed the fighters with cold water, yelling at them. The foreign war cry broke up their fight. United by their fear of the bigger animal, the duo scampered off towards the trash cans in the side yard. We slept.

At daybreak, we stepped outside and found blood stains on the wall. Fauna was speaking again. What might have happened! I had never been more grateful for a wall in my whole life! As the toddler inside and the toddler outside said 'Than U, Bo' (Thank you, Wall), I realized what had happened last night. The recurrent dream of my childhood had visited me like an old uncle. I had to be woken up to record it, remember it and everything that followed. We turned around to walk back to the house, startled by another unusual visitor. A scared opossum. Another creature I had only heard of and read about, right there in my own backyard. She stared and stayed in her corner, not bothering to play dead with those who had lived like ghosts. She stayed there for three days waiting, a messenger with urgent secrets in a language no one understood.

Love so deep that it certainly was not of this earth, fell over me like a waterfall, drenching me with peace so deep that it, too, was not of this earth. But I recognized it. The girl with the skirt of the mysterious glittery fluff. Me.

What was real? And what wasn't? Those questions again! Strangely, I was beginning to get used to this already. I had never lost my mind before. But I had never been so alert, either. Everything seemed so incredibly vibrant! The sky was bluer. The sunlight was brighter. The wildflowers were more vivid. The white noises of the morning were truer. Everything was so magnificently alive! I had been living in layers of thick blankets, and they were now finally off. And the world revealed itself — the good, the bad, and the ugly in full splendour. I felt alive for the first time. Perhaps it was a rebirth. I felt deeply connected to everything and to everyone. From shards of glass and beer spilled on the road, to the road itself, the rows of trash cans, the half-eaten avocados and the squirrels that had tasted them and the trees they now did acrobatics upon and the Earth the trees stood upon. They were not outside of me. Just as much as my fingers and toes and the worms dancing in my tummy were me. I was them. They were I. Everything was me. I and Me. Me and I.

A hummingbird hovered outside the open backyard door. 'In!' Without thinking, without saying one word out aloud, I realized I had just asked it to enter. It was like moving one foot in front of another while walking, without thought or effort. It felt no different from any other part of me. My eyes which were seeing things, my ears which were hearing things and my body which was feeling foreign things. The kitchen's two-in-one whiteness, one known, one unknown was immediately coloured with a two-in-one creature that moved non-stop and stayed still at the same time. Sixteen inches away from my face, it looked straight at me. I stood there transfixed, deeply moved. Each moment too full of life. The construct of time, which I had lost all sense of, seemed like an exercise in defeat. Then just as suddenly, I said 'Out!' Without thinking, without saying one word out aloud, I realized I had just asked it to leave. And it did! It hovered outside the open glass door, until the delicate spell finally broke.

A confederacy of invisible forces was hatching an invisible conspiracy. InPlainSight. I felt like the Hare Rama Hare Krishna types, the hippies and yogis — finally settling into California. Misunderstood and abandoned by the ones who loved me in their own way, frightened by Google in its hometown, I turned desperately to whatever this mysterious force could send to me. Because something was leading me and I surprised myself by following it on autopilot. It was like being in the self-driving car I had seen at a press event. I did not know then that this was how I was going to live. Search after search on Google led me to a strange new word: *kundalini*. Torn between this tug of war of excruciating paranoia and unreal peace, a two-in-one existence where unbelievable things were happening all the time, I was now ready to believe anything. More searches revealed a whole new term, big enough to be a person with a first and a last name. *Kundalini awakening*. So far, I had only heard of *kundalini* as a form of yoga with forceful breathing practiced primarily by Caucasian Sikhs. Search upon search led me to Facebook groups and forums where many had experienced remarkably similar symptoms as mine. It was uncanny that what western medicine saw as a mental illness, New Age spirituality, and some Caucasian Hindu groups that I had judged and consciously avoided over the years like a flu virus saw not only as a gift, but as completely natural.

The Smell of Relief flooded my pulsating body. But there was no incense around. Just like the many things I had been living with which weren't there. Like Alice, I fell down a long rabbit hole into Wonderland. The force guided me to a specific yoga studio amidst the many dotting Mountain View. I drove myself there like a self-driving car. Then it struck me that I had driven myself like a self-driving car in Stanford as well! There was so much of me watching myself. Was life a movie then? Who was I?

All the world's a stage.

And all the men and women merely players.

Another eerie whisper *felt* on my ears and not just as a voice in my head repeated these lines from the Shakespeare play I had studied in high school.

The 78-year-old Ashtanga yoga teacher was dressed in loose, flowy white cotton pants and tunic. We met as though we had an appointment, as if we weren't strangers. I knew she was Persian, she knew I was Indian. How, I still don't know. She welcomed me into her office. Immediately, my extreme anxiety painted the walls. She looked briefly left and right, perhaps noticing the colour change. I don't know why I mechanically listed out my menu of symptoms like a waiter's greeting at a dhaba listing out the foods on offer.

'How can I explain these to a doctor? And which doctor do I even ask for!' She placed her hand over mine with the grandmotherly comfort I had ached for my whole life. 'How can you explain vibrations to a doctor?' she smiled. 'They will think you are mad.' I burst into tears. The room turned maroon. I noticed her card, which said she was a Reiki Master, Life Coach, Healing Touch Practitioner. The first few words I was learning in a whole new vocabulary. (I did not know then that three years later, like her I'd become a Reiki Master and teacher myself, helping people in ways western medicine never could.) She repeated '*kundalini* awakening', the very first term I had so recently learned. Closing her eyes, she held my already pulsating hand. My blood vessels throbbed like a mad heart, threatening to burst out of my skin with this extra force of energy.

'You need "grounding". I see in you a female Ganesha. Is there an Indian goddess like this? It is coming across very strongly.' My head shook in a capital NO, ashamed at my ignorance. 'I'm a non-believer. But now I don't know what to believe in, what is real, what isn't.'

'That doesn't matter because all are illusions,' she said. I smiled.

'I'm going to give my female Ganesha, a Ganesha meditation. Several Ganeshas are sitting in a circle. You're in the middle. They're protecting you. Focus on this as you meditate.' Calm washed over me, rinsing the maroon off the walls.

Without a word, like with the hummingbird, I followed her into the main studio where she was holding a deep relaxation class. My first meditation class, where we lay down with eye pillows filled with buckwheat and lavender. Relaxed with the deep breaths, I realized I had fallen asleep only when she woke me up to pick up a shamanic animal card. I got an elephant.

'What did I say? I'm getting goosebumps!'

At home, I did the Ganesha meditation until it became a visual I could switch to in a blink. To me, Ganesha had just been an archetype like all other gods I saw worshipped. Yet, the power and the protection was incredibly strong. In spite of the sounds and popping in my ears, the indescribable things I continued to see and the otherworldly presences I couldn't prove but knew were there, I finally felt safe. And deeply loved.

A stranger had appeared out of nowhere to cure me. And I was healing. Faster than instant coffee! It was beyond astonishing. By the grace of Google, I knew this was nothing short of a miracle. The internet said there were ample cases of *kundalini* awakenings gone wrong which had landed people in mental asylums with skizzofreneeah. Only shamans (favourite new word) understood what this was.

Soon people would inform me that these were visions, psychic phenomena. And I had experienced the gifts of the Clairs:

1. Clairvoyance (clear seeing)
2. Clairaudience (clear hearing)
3. Clairsentience (clear feeling)
4. Claircognizance (clear knowing)

   And in smaller quantities:

5. Clairgustance (clear tasting)
6. Clairalience (clear smelling)

The paranormal had become normal. The supernatural had become natural. The mundane and the magical had merged. Amidst my human family, lived a bunch of dream creatures, just as real. Dream creatures who could not be distilled into the words of mortals. Dream creatures I tried to first categorize into human labels but soon learned to recognize them by their essence instead, which could not be put into human words. A stout medieval man whose closest resemblance would be to a Viking, stared outside my window in deep thought, as if he were staring not at my neighbour's fence, but into the sea he would sail into. Realizing that I had noticed him, he stopped all of a sudden to stare at me. I froze in fear! What dimension was I in? He disappeared. Another heavyset, wider but still tall creature with a fat skeleton face was walking towards me. He was absolutely chilling! Ma, who had died of leukemia six years ago wafted through dreams and realities like a dream herself. The privileges of being a ghost! The WalkingBreathingDead. Other dead relatives made appearances too. My husband's grandmother Biji, my grandmother Thamma and my son's would-have-been-grandmother Amaar Maa with a white and brown Himalayan sheepdog at her neck. Years later, Pup-Pa would tell me this was Big Mother's pet from Assam who had loved Amaar Maa. Hybrid animal spirits, half hippo-half horse, free-spirited, giant, shiny creatures who looked like unicorns, whales without eyelids who stared and sang, snakes who were as affectionate as Labradors... And these were the creatures and visions I could describe. Was this what an LSD trip felt like? Like the Cheshire Cat, they shifted into bits and pieces, appearing and disappearing. An endless peekaboo of puzzle pieces. Archetypes of Hindu gods made cameo appearances, behaving like no myth had ever taught me. In fact, it took me a few seconds to place them. A very happy figure danced through the matter that was my head, as if it didn't exist. I realized this was Krishna. An unbelievably stunning ten-foot-tall blue woman swung wildly from the tree branches. She was restless. She had the playfulness, gentleness and mischief of a child, yet she loved like a mother. It took me a while to register this vision of Kali. Nothing like what I had seen in comic books or in religious art. A terribly malnourished-looking man, tall and skinny as a stick, appeared in a swimming pool as infinite as the ocean, smiling, more tranquil than the waters around him. It took me a few seconds to register that this was Shiva. His peace put me at peace. The scary figures disappeared. Tall, shadowy figures which looked like they were made of light blue X-rays surrounded me. The ones who had rescued me at the swimming pool. I knew them at once! They drenched me in a waterfall of love so unconditional, that it couldn't be of this world. These extremely benevolent beings were extraterrestrial guides, angels. Nothing like anything I had ever seen. I knew that these were my perceptions. If I were to perceive them like those conditioned by religion, like worshippers and believers, perhaps they might have appeared like they did in religious art. But how did I know these answers instantly? From where were they coming? How were they appearing even faster than a Google search?

Meditations and self-hypnosis sessions on YouTube made me calmer. But they took me to insane places. Purple oceans with popsicle sands. Cities with tall buildings made of gems and crystals. Lush rainforests with rivers and waterfalls on high snowy mountains which merged into the sky. Outer space was a riot of colours right where I was. Crawling in the bark of a tree, where I was both bark and human skin. Swimming in air, in a purple universe. The ring of a planet that looked like Saturn, going through my head, vapour mixing with vapour. Endless stretches of outer space! I did not know what was more addictive. That these were a vending machine of insane beauty and temporary but instant peace? Or that these psychedelic trips gave me experiences movies and virtual reality never could? I was hooked! Like a drug addict. Perhaps this is why people get hooked on drugs. Naturally, normal earthly travel lost its appeal. But I connected with Mother Earth in a way I didn't know was possible, like a foetus to its womb.

I had no doubt that we were all consciousness, not just the ones in human bodies but also those in apparently non-living things. I finally grasped the meaning of soul. Old words came alive with new meanings, some for the first time. The world was indeed an illusion, a reflection of our inner reality, each moment, a moment of birth and death. I felt like I was walking on air, unable to feel the ground beneath my feet. Soon enough, I found a way to be grounded, finding them in all kinds of things like divination tools like crystals, angels, gods, goddesses, oracle cards... My favourite became tarot cards with their beautiful medieval archetypes. I used them and others as tools to go within myself for answers or to feel better, needing less and less validation from the external world.

My world collapsed as easily as the Lego block towers my toddler loved building so much. My closest friendships metamorphosed, faded away or ended altogether. Completely new ones replaced them. Conversations with strangers, some of them with cashiers and waiters, were strangely warm. Pretences became impossible. The business book I was working on collapsed mysteriously. My new phone went off, just like that. Some electronic items sparked, then finally went dead. Often, they did not return to life — not for a while. My sciatica miraculously healed itself. My contract with the publication I was supposed to join fell through at the last minute. Obligations and people were shed off like snakeskin. I was seen as a snake. Like a snake, I couldn't have cared less. A perfect synchronicity. This would be my second favourite new word after 'energy'. I had begun to see everything as energy. I got into meditations where I could project light to shift to whatever energy I wanted to manifest within me.

PART V

FREEDOM

19

The Lemon and the Elephant

Children and animals know obvious truths. InPlainSight truths. Truths that escape grown-ups altogether. Only because grown-ups unconsciously live in conditioned webs of hand-me-down narratives. My childhood self knew that reality was a private affair. Truth was not absolute but an infinite rainbow of endless colours. The Homeless Peacock/Water Phoenix were my reality. Nobody else saw this. Just like they did not see the Tentacle which lived in a girl who lived in books. Grown-uphood meant losing the wisdom which had always been mine. An unconscious trade off in the quest for a few drops of power. Or which, like the countless grown-ups who didn't understand what true power was, I thought was power.

It 2.0 might not have caused much trouble to the little girl by the pet peepul who had met with X-ray beings, a tribe of monkeys, one panther, one pet toad, a mongoose on a wall by a graveyard, an owl doctor. But It 2.0 decided to happen in grown-uphood, too. Perhaps that's exactly why. My rational adult mind, sharpened even further towards logic, was still messed up. What then was reality? What was truth?

I could not tamely succumb to the dogma of religion. And even as I made a career out of interviewing scientists and the biggest minds in Silly Con Valley, I found myself not yet ready to accept the dogma of modern science either. It was different from how Archimedes had had his Eureka moment. Or how the apple fell even for the father of modern science. There was an epiphanic quality to their discoveries which seemed lost in the righteousness that I saw in most scientists. Like the Tentacle, fragments of the Railway Princess lived on in me, like the many wounded inner children who live on in grown-ups. I had turned this scepticism and wonder (a two-in-one) into a career. So how then, could I simply accept all New Age beliefs? I knew I could accept only my own truth, while remaining open to observations and experimentation like science had taught me. It dawned on me then that by modern standards, I had mastered the art of waiting. The panther had left its feline dewdrops on me. I became a cat by a window, waiting and watching, without expectation. Okay with whatever happened, even if it was nothing. Drenched in the okayness of another OkayRainCloud, it returned. The peace by the pet peepul. The Feeling of Wholeness.

Sensing the lack of resistance in this newfound sense of peace, the many creatures I had no template to place became irrelevant, like walls and tables. Them being there or not there depended primarily on the attention I gave to them. I did not know then that such seemingly disconnected results would become routine. Just as mysteriously, a new law flowed around my beliefs, like water flows around rocks, and centred itself into my life, as certain and sensible as the law of gravity. The Law of

Attraction. It essentially said that one's external reality mirrors one's inner reality and that we were magnets of what we believed we were. *Thoughts create your reality* — a phrase that I encountered again and again in different forms with the same certainty as the Tentacle. I wish somebody had told me about this before. My whole life might have been different. I wish this simple phrase was taught to children in schools. I didn't know then that three years later, I'd begin doing just that, sneaking in this superpower of knowledge into the children around me, telling them that they controlled their reality. And watch them blossom — like I wish I had.

New Agers had two favourite analogies:

1. *The Lemon:* Think of a lemon squeezed in your mouth and you'll be able to taste it, even salivate, in spite of the fact that it isn't there. This proves a two-in-one secret: That the subconscious mind is king and yet it cannot distinguish between what's real and what isn't. It's like when you watch a horror film and are terrified even though you know what you are watching is just a film. My abuse had ended many years ago, but my mind had made it so important and relevant that it lived on in me for decades, manifesting the original trauma again and again in completely irrelevant situations. That's why reality is so tricky. It explained why I'd given up on little things, and given up so easily, because I was completely consumed, completely drained with the invisible, the Tentacle.

Reality depends upon the meanings we ascribe to things because, by themselves, they have no meaning. And human beings are the only species that do this non-stop. My fears gave Ganesha a meaning it never had before for me. The more I meditated, the more I observed, the more I saw things for what they were, stripped of all their connotations. Foods weren't tasty or tasteless. Heirlooms weren't treasured. Things weren't beautiful or ugly. Activities weren't fun or torture. People weren't lovable or unlovable. Countries, cults, groups and religions weren't safe or dangerous. These were all meanings we had coloured them with. Meanings which were often a result of deliberate conditioning from early childhood by caregivers, teachers, peers, society, media and culture, but also often based on subconscious decisions made by us for being 'good'. Reading, writing, being gentle and an easy kid got me praise and zero complaints. So, I had decided these were 'good' — and consequently, their opposites were bad — and made a life out of it.

What if I had chosen the opposite? The path more popular: of toughness and survival instead of gentleness and vulnerability? What if I had chosen to be assertive and aggressive instead of being a people-pleaser? Like the intimidating women I kept meeting and was triggered by.

I found my way to Teal Swan, a teacher just one year younger than me, who, with her badass, zero-bullshit approach after escaping a childhood of unbelievable, ghastly Satanic ritual abuse, became my favourite teacher. She called meaning 'the self-destruct button' and explained that one could step into a new dawn once we had befriended and integrated into ourselves what Jungian psychology called 'shadows' — aspects we had given meaning to as being bad and therefore rejected and by which we were triggered. Like Jung and Nietzsche whom I had read on Platform No. 4, Swan showed me that a fulfilling life was possible this way. The difference was that unlike them, she was a living example of someone who had suffered unimaginable trauma (including childhood sexual abuse) and still, found a fulfilling life. If it was possible for her, it was possible for anybody, including me. But you had to live a life in which every single decision, including the simplest ones boiled down to: What would someone who loved themselves do? This was harder than it sounded. One day, it was watching Netflix and eating chips; the other day it was eating raw fruits and vegetables and finishing goals I had procrastinated on; another day it was self-loving to banish kale and a BFF from my life. It boiled down to simple inane things like saying 'no' to visiting a friend because parking there was a nightmare and would paint my day maroon in anxiety and overwhelm me. Another day it was about doing exactly that. Because we are never finished, what this did was make me live in flow, trusting myself in a way I never had before — that I had my own back and that I had endless choices.

The most important thing I learned from Swan was a form of an 'emotional vipassana' (which she later developed into a process and a book called *The Completion Process*). My own interpretation, a medley, began with scanning my body, something that hours of meditation and life as a Watcher have made instant, and seeing what feeling manifested as what sensation in the body. That's what emotion is in the body: the physical translation of a feeling. Things like the Smell of Relief, the Feeling of Love, Shame and Anxiety. When did I last feel this way? When did I first feel this way? The questions made me live my life backwards, and as I answered each question, the core trauma shifted deeper and deeper into the past. To my utter shock, the Tentacle was not my core trauma! It was the feeling of extreme vulnerability, powerlessness, rejection and abandonment when Maa died, when Pup-Pa never showed up. Deeper and deeper, I went until one day in a deep meditative state, I travelled to the time when I was a foetus in Amaar Maa's womb. I felt everything the foetus and my dead original mother felt simultaneously, like Me had felt I. Maa's fear, her rejection, her not wanting me, things that so many women of her generation (and today) weren't allowed to express even to themselves. I realized how like millions I was born into invisible trauma InPlainSight.

All my life I had felt weak, defenseless, vulnerable to almost everything, like a fragile fledgling that had fallen out of its mama's nest. My reality attracted exactly those things to match my emotions — abandonment, rejection, the feeling of being unlovable, bullying, abuse. And I had remained completely focused on this awful reality, thereby attracting even more abuse, completely unaware that I was not powerless. That it was in my power to create my own reality, that I could shift it with a mere change of focus. I suddenly realized how drowning myself in books had literally saved my life! Every single time I escaped into the world of books, I had stopped this momentum and shifted focus from my lifelong pity party (that was sometimes subconscious, sometimes unconscious, often conscious as reflected by the *Maahaara* sympathy I received). Consequently, creating the space to allow other fresh energies — the good things (UndiagnosedAutisticUncle, boarding school, escaping abuse, wonderful friends, a loving husband and a magical child) to flow through.

2. *The Elephant:* Baby elephants are often tied to tree trunks with thin ropes. When they grow up, they have no idea that they're so mighty that they can uproot the tree and set themselves free with a mere pull. This means that the mind is the greatest muscle, where all the power resides. The power to stay chained up or the power to set you free.

I had been one such baby elephant chained by a Tentacle. But now as a grown-up, I had the power to smash the Tentacle, throw out the meaning I had given to it, which had allowed it to rule my life, and set myself free. It really was that simple. Having practically raised myself, I finally decided to parent myself. When I looked around me, I saw that it didn't really matter whether people were raised in dysfunctional or normal families, in war zones or peaceful areas, everybody was wounded. Because modern society spells isolation, a lack of connection, where independence is encouraged whereas interdependence is the rule of Mother Nature. And in this alienation, lies the original wound.

Everything is a story, my parent-self told my child-self. I can shift my narrative at any time. Why let someone else choose my story? Life after all is a buffet of endless essences and energies. Everything is energy. We are all magnets. We can shift any time, consciously choosing our energies and consequently the ones we actually want to attract.

As I changed my own narrative, I felt lighter. By getting out of my own way, the invisible tigers in the room disappeared. By changing my old negative self-talk and replacing them with affirmations, my life transformed. My strained familial relations healed. I felt lovable in this reality like I had in the ethers. Support streamed in from the ethers, this reality, from everywhere like the new law that had flowed in, like water flows around rocks. But I was still not as free as a waterfall.

I had to free myself because I was the only one who could. But how?

How could I be free? Completely free? 'Through forgiveness,' the autopilot voice said. Logic told me it was my subconscious spouting the Christian beliefs taught in my boarding school. Magic told me it was a chorus of my friends in the ethers, angels and spirit guides.

This world is duality. Yin and yang, love and hate, giving and receiving, male and female, failure and success, good and evil, freedom and terrorism, war and peace. It didn't matter. If we were both living and dying at the same time, could I then, not live in both magic and logic together? Ultimately, they said the same thing. A battle which was unnecessary and which could be transcended by not fighting at all, by simply observing, acknowledging and validating both as truths. Very soon, I was led to Ho'oponopono — the Hawaiian prayer of forgiveness:

I am sorry.
Please forgive me.
Thank you.
I love you.

The Tentacle grabbed my trachea, gagging me. I threw up, startling my toddler. Fascinated, he watched the floor, hypnotized by the yucky green paint on the white linoleum.

'What would someone who loved themselves do?' a voice insisted. (Logic said it was the new belief I had sowed within. Magic said it was one of my guides, talking to me through my intuition. Again, both said the same thing.) While cleaning the kitchen, calming down, composing myself, I said again and again:

I am sorry.
Please forgive me.
Thank you.
I love you.

Devastated, a tsunami of tears drenched me and the floor. The toddler grabbed a diaper like he often did to contain liquid messes. 'Mummum diapo,' he said. The white kitchen tiles of a rented house in Mountain View, home to Google, where a little sea had formed out of Google searches. A sea of tears which finally drowned a tentacle.

The Tentacle was dead.

20

Dinner with the Rapist

Whiteness, the dazzling whiteness I had gotten used to, white which was golden but so bright that it looked white, flooded everything, becoming everything, until it was all that there was. White floor, white table, white chair, white nothingness, white everythingness. The shapes and matters were imaginary, illusory playthings. Thirty years later, I was having dinner with my original rapist. I had spent decades dreading him. The mere thought of being in his presence, even on the phone, let alone in person, would send a shudder rippling through me, making me tremble like walls shaking during an earthquake. And here he was now, on the chair across the long dining table. The man who had written the blueprint of my life and then, passed on the pen to others to continue doing so. But had he? Had they? Or had I given them that right? I was tired of running. Fed up of living in a cage. It was time for closure. It was time to return home.

A fat black gecko appeared, a striking contrast to the ethereal whitewash. Reflecting all my fears, a real-life version of the recently departed Tentacle, this shadow animal watched me cautiously with beady eyes that gave nothing away.

When I looked closely, I could barely recognize him. Was this really P? He was nothing like the P I knew. His shoulders slouched, his head crouched, P was now the very picture of defeat. If Shame were a person, his surname would be P. He couldn't bear to lift up his head, leave alone look me in the eye. The most broken man I knew. So frail! More shadow than man. Was this the creature I'd given decades of my life away to? I could have killed him with a mere push and a stomp of the three-inch white heels that had somehow wrapped around my feet. The old me, pre-It 2.0 might just have. But I wasn't the old me anymore. I did not know who I was. But I knew I was not my story. I was not my abuse. I was not my suffering. I was so much more than all of my roles, my joys, and certainly more than my imprisonment.

I am sorry.
Please forgive me.
Thank you.
I love you.

P burst into tears, refusing to look up. I melted in pity, feeling sorry for him. How powerless! How out of touch with their own humanity and inherent innocence people can be to stoop so low as to get a high by raping a child? I was not condoning his act. No way! Simply seeing him, out of his human story, the same way that I had decided I was not my story.

The ethers turned into a concert of sobs, soft sobs balancing loud wails. A two-in-one rhythm simultaneously soothing and eerie. It wasn't just P. Into him had merged a hand, a hand of horror. The Hand! That had been so horrific that the child it consumed had to abandon her body. Then came a dark face. An incredibly shocking human face. Because it was made up not of skin but of peeling barks. I knew it! I knew those peels! My fragile guava tree's supernatural bark, peeling off endlessly like injured skin, making its hidden magical properties crystal clear. It was S Sir. The peels turned into a yellow rectangle, a cement sign on a railway platform, a name which began to reverse-evaporate random letter by random letter into existence. M...A...H... An ethereal word game. D...I...H... Painful pinches on my skin, A...G. My body remembered. D...N... GandhiGandhidham Uncle! An amalgamation of faces known and unknown, which my emotional *vipassana*-trained body translated immediately. Faster than a Google search. Fear in my throat, a tightening of my chest muscles, a pain building there, a feeling of dizziness. Memories of an animal prey the body had stored. Only she did not know the predators were their own prey. The process repeated. The crushed souls were not souls but smithereens. Fragments of self-hate.

A soft, velvety warm hug landed on my shoulders, the weight of feathers washing me with the Feeling of Love. Pure and unconditional. Calm filled me, all of my human self, from above my scalp to below my toes. I turned around. A gigantic dragon face. It looked at me with fierce, kind ruby eyes. I felt like I was looking at myself. Me looking at I. I had a beak. I knew this creature from my own myth. I had met it before. A dragon bird so big that a lake could not contain it. In its embrace, I was the size of a puppy. It had the weight of feathers because it had feathers. Feathers so brilliant, I couldn't place them. I thought of the colours I knew so I could make a memory. Purple. And blue. And fuchsia. And gold. So much gold! A golden halo which turned the ethereal white golden. 'Ho'oponopono' — its velvety whisper danced in my ear canal, turning into tickles.

I am sorry.
Please forgive me.
Thank you.
I love you.

I smiled, realizing I had finally set myself free. The gecko disappeared, taking the alloy of assaulters away with it. The room was golden. This must be Heaven, I thought. 'Yes, it is in you,' ran the tickle. The Water Phoenix said goodbye with its eyes and disappeared. On my arms, it left some of its golden halo dust. My skin glowed translucent, cool to the touch, not warm. Because it was a water phoenix, not a firebird, which had turned it so. I knew this feeling. The foreign coolness of Me's world on my glowing translucent skin.

21

I Am Not My Story: Life as Art

The secrets of this world lie in the ethers. I am no exception. What had happened in the ethers had changed everything. The glow I radiated now lit up my life in unimaginable ways. Freedom filled my life. The kinder I was, the kinder the world was. The more I believed in myself, the more the world reflected that. Not so long ago, it was the opposite. I hated myself without knowing it and the world reflected just that. Now, I saw in myself love, acceptance, safety and celebration. That's what the world reflects. A new life! But how many times had I died before this rebirth? To remember who we are, we have to first forget who we have been. That blank slate is the only way to discovery, to creation.

When I look back at It 2.0, I realize that what happened to me (and the countless others, many of whom shared their stories online) is a reflection of what is happening to society today — a complete breakdown of all the systems that held meaning in the past, to make way for a new world. My esoteric journey of healing had simple, logical roots in extreme depression. The final straw had been my post-partum depression. Like so many invisible truths InPlainSight, it had gone undiagnosed. Each case is different. I had been able to bond with my baby. But the pain of this last bout of depression upon the already unbearable heavy luggage I was carrying had been too much. In esoteric circles, my *kundalini* awakening would be interpreted as simply 'emotional suicide'. There are several other bodies — the ethereal, emotional, mental, astral, light, etc. beyond the physical body — and that explains just how I had felt beyond my toes and scalp. It was my emotional body that had been defeated by a life of self-sabotage. I had died before I had died. That's why unlike those in deep meditation to awaken their *kundalinis*, my *kundalini* awakening had been spontaneous and scary. I attracted all I had been. Today, I know that *kundalini* is not a hippie concept but simply life force energy, which is everywhere, in everything. It is most obvious in the laughter of children, in the serenity of nature, and in the nourishment of animals. What mystics call the natural state of living in 'pure bliss'. A simple concept when you live each present moment completely, as it is devoid of the lenses of the past or the future, resisting nothing. Naturally, this also means dying every minute to the past. This state is so perfect, it defies words. There's such peace that it makes happiness appear shallow.

Life is art. The greatest art there is. What happened does not matter. What matters today is what you do with the past. When you let go of your story and live in the *now*, infinite possibilities show up. Paint each moment with new colours, new choices, be whoever you choose to be, devoid of roles and imposed identities. Like my son Reyo who is Batman now, a pirate later, a wolf, then a sheep…

When did we lose this wisdom which we were born with, which was always ours?

That is how I transcended a life of abuse. I released all that struggle, that bitterness. I reclaimed my life, not with strength and survival but with gentleness and forgiveness. Like Letitia.

Devil No. 1 and I had a falling out in our adult years. Devil No. 2 and M and I are close. Dinner with P is due whenever I'm in his city. Forgiveness is the most selfish choice you can make. It is the most self-loving choice you can make. Forgiveness is the last step but you cannot rush or force it. You cannot just wake up one morning and decide to forgive. Contrary to the pressure in spiritual circles, it cannot and must not be forced. That wouldn't be self-loving, would it? You can only forgive when you are ready. Forgiveness often comes naturally when you have healed enough to truly know your Own Power and realize that there is nothing left to forgive. Why? Because it isn't about the abuser at all. It is the only way to fill the void within you, no matter the trauma. And so it is often the only choice that works. It takes a minute and a simple decision to shift. (But this state of resolution arrives only after a lot of healing — including physically distancing one's self from the abuser — has already taken place.)

What happened doesn't matter, what matters is what you do with it. With the power of awareness, we alchemize suffering into gold. We realize that no matter our stories, no matter how great our suffering, freedom is in our hands.

A simple decision, one devoid of overthinking. The psychologist Barry Schwartz said, 'Analysis is paralysis.' This is exactly what I had been doing, pretty much like everyone I knew. Till I was lost at sea, in a sea of questions, in a sea of stories to torture myself with. By embracing the way in which Mother Nature, little children (because they are still relatively less conditioned) and animals live, without over-analyzing, I found my way to the Taoist concept of Wu Wei — action through inaction. I now live in flow. I never get writer's block.

Each moment you live your truth as a wholesome, integrated being (shadows, horns, beaks, feathers, tails and all), knowing that it will shift the next, you know you are living your life as art. It's as if the whole universe is whispering its stories, showering me in love that I didn't believe was possible on earth. Is this happiness, Heaven on earth? Is this enlightenment? I don't know. And I don't care. Why add labels? Why add the burden of meaning?

Today I am free, as free as the little girl whose first love was a tree.

Perhaps this is what the peepul and the animals who turned life into magic realism had always been trying to tell me. It took me three decades to realize what was always there.

When the storm comes, I go into the eye of the storm, surrendering, offering myself to it, letting it rip me apart, consume me... Because I am not fighting the storms, not resisting them, their strength gets lesser and lesser. By befriending the dragon, I tamed it. Today, I see panic and peace, depression and joy as energies, as natural as the rising and falling of tides, as certain as the cycles of the seasons, each with its own beauty.

Manga Kaka was wrong. My pet peepul was not the tree of death. It was the tree of life. Perhaps this is why, unknown to the grown-up the little girl lived inside, she sought out a tree outside her bedroom window, no matter where she lived in the world. Once it was a group of skinny nameless trees that lived as one, swaying in the wind — tipsy aunties at a party. Witnesses to bloody raccoon battles, toddlers blossoming, opossum messengers. Another time, it was a grandmother orange tree, which lit up the unbearable gloom of the grey winter sky with its hundred splendid suns. Once, it was the blazing beauty of a red maple showering Big Mother vermillion love. Another time, it was a flowering dogwood tree which wouldn't let you focus on anything.

Today, a family of redwoods watch over me from my bedroom window. Mommy redwood, Daddy redwood and a rather grown Baby redwood. On them are many squirrels who use its branches as houses and playgrounds, who prefer cheese pizza and toast even as they bounce in a lake of acorns, which they sometimes dig into treasure holes in the ground, like dogs burying bones, stealthily, making sure nobody is watching.

I lie under these Trees of Life with my son, who is as smitten with them like I once was with another tree. The harsh Californian sun, a photographer's delight, is blinding. It orders us to shut our eyes. I obey, surrendering to its nourishing warmth. It takes me high, high above. I know this place. The topmost part of my peepul, where the leaves were made of gold, gold merging into a lake of liquid golden sunlight so bright that it blinded those who dared to look. I knew this place. I had found the liquid realm. This was my house. I looked at Me. I was the water phoenix. I always was.

[ENDS]

Acknowledgements

All names in this book, except for those of the stray dogs in the railway colony and those visiting the Ancestral House, have been changed.

Throughout this memoir, Lewis Carroll's *Alice in Wonderland* has been mentioned as a heavy influence. The following lines have been quoted from it:

- 'I knew who I was this morning, but I have changed a few times since then.'
- 'You may have noticed I'm not all there by myself.'
- 'It's no use going back to yesterday, because I was a different person then.'
- 'I am not crazy. My reality is just different from yours.'

Characters from *Alice in Wonderland* have been referred to in the following lines:

- 'Did this mean that like Alice and Homeless Peacock/Water Phoenix, I too, lived between worlds?'
- 'Squeezing my eyes open and shut as Alice might have, I waited to discover what lay behind the door with bated breath. Prepared for storage, ready for Wonderland.'

- 'Within minutes of our friendship, I turned them into characters in my stories where they accompanied me on adventures like Alice.'
- 'Like Alice who had grown too tall and too short, too quick?'
- 'Like Alice, I fell down a long rabbit hole into Wonderland.'
- 'Like the Cheshire Cat. Like the Homeless Peacock/ Water Phoenix. No wonder I felt like a ghost!'
- 'She gave me a Cheshire Cat smile.'
- 'Finally having my own house gave me Cheshire Cat grins. Which soon disappeared in bits like the Cheshire Cat until the joy wasn't there.'
- 'Like the Cheshire Cat, they shifted into bits and pieces, appearing and disappearing.'
- 'Freezing, I took a deep puff from my purple pipe!'

Characters and places from *Gulliver's Travels* by Jonathan Swift have been referred to as follows:

- 'I set up home in a corner of their living rooms with my books, travelling to Lilliput, Brobdingnag and Laputa with Gulliver.'
- 'I wished to travel to the land of the Houyhnhnms, the talking horses that Gulliver had visited and, like him, I did not wish to return.'

This sentence has been quoted from *The Castaway*, a short story by Rabindranath Tagore: 'Life was made up of eatings and beatings, and that the beatings largely predominated.'

Lastly, the line, 'All the world's a stage and all the men and women merely players,' has been quoted from the celebrated speech in Act II of the play *As You Like It* by William Shakespeare.

Writing is always an act of courage, but even more so, when one is writing about one's own life. A book like this, therefore, could not have been possible without a group of people, whom I'd like to thank. My immense gratitude to my dear friend and super-agent, the fearless and mighty Kanishka Gupta. Thank you for believing in this book and for making it happen. You are amazing! I am deeply thankful to my generous, kind and patient publisher Prerna Vohra and to Bloomsbury for publishing this book. My editor Reena Singh for her deeply thoughtful edits, thank you. The lovely marketing and publicity team at Bloomsbury, thank you!

Anees Salim, you are a gift: thank you for your elegance, kindness and munificence.

Jerry Pinto, for your big heart, your brilliance and your guidance, *shukriya*.

Devi S. Laskar, I remain grateful for your compassion, consideration and generosity. Thank you!

My magical boy Reyo, I immensely appreciate you letting me steal your summer break to finish this book and for sitting by my side reading happily as I did so, interrupting every two minutes to share something of earth-shattering importance. Thank you also for drowning my computer, for volunteering your priceless 'editing' services (replacing my vocabulary and spelling with your versions), for your endless encouragement, infinite love, wisdom, wit and laughter. You were six years old then, almost the same age where this book kicks off. Thank you for bringing back how I saw the world then, which is uncannily so much like how you do! With you, childhood has returned a second time, and this time it truly is Eden. You remain my inspiration, my favourite author-illustrator and the reason I live.

My husband Rajat, thank you for making my world and everything in it possible. Thank you for bearing with my emergencies of needing to stop the world and disappearing briefly to take down notes or for days to write. Thank you for driving for hours to and fro to ensure Fussypants's babysitting and playdates so that I could write in peace without his editorial interventions. Quoisey, *dhonobaad*! You are the world's best listener.

Amrita Chatterji, *grazie mille* dear sister for believing that I could and insisting that I should write this book when it first came to me. Thank you Baba for being so authentic, for never pretending things were fine when they were not and for showing me very early on in life that parents are imperfect humans, thereby setting both of us free. It was the biggest lesson I learned, which helped me write. Thank you Mummy and Papa for your grace, support and love. In an imperfect world, you are perfection personified. I don't know what I'd do without you.

Muchos gracias to my Indian family in California — Amrita, Mukti, Anand, Shveta, Varun, Rachna, Mukul, Bhatia, Mili, Khandu, Adot, Trisha, Shashank, Vijaya and

Gunjan — for your unconditional love and support. Thank you Jha Uncle and Aunty for babysitting Fussypants.

Bethany Gracias, Sameera Tak, Mittal Solanki — thank you for your eternal love and entertainment, both equally necessary. My dearest friend Anahita Mukherjee, thank you for believing in me, in this book and for ensuring I wrote it. Thank you Saman Usman for your faith and gentleness. Thank you to my writer's group Shut Up and Write Silicon Valley. Thank you Amira, Amy, Aditi, Kelly and Catherine. *Mahalo,* Tiffany — for sending procrastination on a vacation. Kaila Tova, thank you for being such an inspiration and for saying, 'I believe in you!' — which is all one needs.

Thank you Mission Branch Library, Santa Clara, for being the most perfect neighbourhood library, full of light, beautiful picture windows, research books, kind and generous staff and for being right opposite my house! Also, Santa Clara University for being generous enough to let locals come in to research, write and borrow books in your wonderful library. Thank you to the family of redwoods outside my window and its squirrel tenants and hummingbird nests, allowing me to write in full flow. Thank you Ketlee for being the perfect, quiet, sweet neighbourhood cafe for writer groups to write in. Thanks to all of you, I didn't need a writer's retreat.

Gratitude, Peder B. Helland, Spirit Tribe Awakening, Vortex Success, Calm Whale, The Infinite Cup and Ludovico Einaudi for your divine music which made it possible to focus and write in a house full of children. Immense gratitude from the bottom of my healed heart to the many people whose work made my own journey of healing and forgiveness and consequently, made this very book possible: Carl Jung, especially his work on shadows and archetypes, Byron Katie for her process The Work, Eckhart Tolle for *The Power of Now*, Bentinho Massaro and the greatest gratitude to the teacher of authenticity, Teal Swan.

And thank you dearest reader. If you too, had your childhood stolen, I hope this book helps you remember who you are — a magical being who is here to live a magnificent life. You are why this book was written.